EDUCATION OF CHARACTER

EDUCATION OF CHARACTER

Bertrand Russell

Philosophical Library

New York, N. Y.

CONTENTS

INTRODUCTION

THERE must be in the world many parents who, like the present author, have young children whom they are anxious to educate as well as possible, but reluctant to expose to the evils of most existing educational institutions. The difficulties of such parents are not soluble by any effort on the part of isolated individuals. It is of course possible to bring up children at home by means of governesses and tutors, but this plan deprives them of the companionship which their nature craves, and without which some essential elements of education must be lacking. Moreover it is extremely bad for a boy or girl to be made to feel "odd" and different from other boys and girls: this feeling, when traced to parents as its cause, is almost certain to rouse resentment against them, leading to a love of all that they most dislike. The conscientious parent may be driven by these considerations to send his boys and girls to schools in which he sees grave defects, merely because no existing schools seem to him satisfactory—or, if any are satisfactory, they are not in his neighbourhood. Thus the cause of educational reform is forced upon conscientious parents, not only for the good of the community, but also for the good of their own children. If the parents are well-to-do, it is not necessary to the solution of their private problem that *all* schools should be good, but only that there should be some good school geographically available. But for wage-earning parents nothing suffices except reform in the elementary schools. As one parent will object to the reforms which another parent desires, nothing will serve except an energetic educational propaganda, which is not likely to prove effective until long after the reformer's children are grown up. Thus from love for our own children we are driven, step by step, into the wider sphere of politics and philosophy.

From this wider sphere I desire, in the following pages, to remain aloof as far as possible. The greater part of what I have to say will not be dependent upon the views that I may happen to hold as regards the major controversies of our age. But *complete* independence in this regard is impossible. The education we desire for our children must depend upon our ideals of human character, and our hopes as to the part they are to play in the community. A pacifist will not desire for his children the education which seems good to a militarist; the educational outlook of a communist will not be

the same as that of an individualist. To come
to a more fundamental cleavage: there can be
no agreement between those who regard education as a means of instilling certain definite beliefs and those who think that it should produce
the power of independent judgment. Where
such issues are relevant, it would be idle to
shirk them. At the same time, there is a considerable body of new knowledge in psychology
and pedagogy which is independent of these
ultimate questions, and has an intimate bearing
on education. Already it has produced very
important results, but a great deal remains to
be done before its teachings have been fully
assimilated. This is especially true of the first
five years of life; these have been found to have
an importance far greater than that formerly
attributed to them, which involves a corre-
sponding increase in the educational importance of parents. My aim and purpose, wherever possible, will be to avoid controversial
issues. Polemical writing is necessary in some
spheres; but in addressing parents one may
assume a sincere desire for the welfare of their
offspring, and this alone, in conjunction with
modern knowledge, suffices to decide a very
large number of educational problems. What
I have to say is the outcome of perplexities in
regard to my own children; it is therefore not
remote or theoretical, and may, I hope, help to

clarify the thoughts of other parents faced with a like perplexity, whether in the way of agreement with my conclusions or the opposite. The opinions of parents are immensely important, because, for lack of expert knowledge, parents are too often a drag upon the best educationists. If parents desire a good education for their children, there will, I am convinced, be no lack of teachers willing and able to give it.

I propose, in what follows, to consider first the aims of education: the kind of individuals, and the kind of community, that we may reasonably hope to see produced by education applied to raw material of the present quality. I ignore the question of the improvement of the breed, whether by eugenics or by any other process, natural or artificial, since this is essentially outside the problems of education. But I attach great weight to modern psychological discoveries which tend to show that character is determined by early education to a much greater extent than was thought by the most enthusiastic educationists of former generations. I distinguish between education of character and education in knowledge, which may be called instruction in the strict sense. The distinction is useful, though not ultimate: some virtues are required in a pupil who is to become instructed, and much knowledge is required for

8

the successful practice of many important virtues. For purposes of discussion, however, instruction can be kept apart from education of character. The further education which men and women derive from life and the world I shall regard as lying outside my scope; but to make men and women capable of learning from experience should be one of the aims which early education should keep most prominently in view.

THE first year of life was formerly regarded as lying outside the sphere of education. At least until the infant could speak, if not longer, it was left to the entirely unchecked care of mothers and nurses, who were supposed to know by instinct what was good for the child. As a matter of fact, they did not know. An enormous proportion of children died during the first year, and of the remainder many were already ruined in health. By bad handling, the foundations had been laid for disastrous habits of mind. All this has only recently been realized. The invasion of the nursery by science is often resented, because it disturbs the sentimental picture of mother and child. But sentimentality and love cannot coexist; the parent who loves his or her child will wish it to live, even if it should be necessary to employ intelligence for the purpose. Accordingly we find this sentimentality strongest in childless people and in people who, like Rousseau, are willing to leave their children to the Foundling

Hospital. Most educated parents are eager to know what science has to say, and uneducated parents, also, learn from maternity centres. The result is shown in the remarkable diminution of infant mortality. There is reason to think that, with adequate care and skill, very few children would die in infancy. Not only would few die, but the survivors would be healthier in mind and body.

Questions of physical health, strictly speaking, lie outside the scope of this book, and must be left to medical practitioners. I shall touch on them only where they have psychological importance. But physical and mental are scarcely distinguishable in the first year of life. Moreover the educator in later years may find himself handicapped by purely physiological mistakes in handling the infant. We cannot therefore altogether avoid trespassing upon ground which does not of right belong to us.

The new-born infant has reflexes and instincts, but no habits. Whatever habits it may have acquired in the womb are useless in its new situation: even breathing sometimes has to be taught, and some children die because they do not learn the lesson quickly enough. There is one well-developed instinct, the instinct of sucking; when the child is engaged in this occupation, it feels at home with its new environment. But the rest of its waking life is passed in a vague bewilderment, from which relief is found by sleeping most of the twenty-four hours. At the end of a fortnight, all this is changed. The child has acquired expectations from regularly recurring experiences. It is already a conservative—probably a more complete conservative than at any later time. Any novelty is met with resentment. If it could speak, it would say: "Do you suppose I am going to change the habits of a lifetime at my time of life?" The rapidity with which infants acquire habits is amazing. Every bad habit acquired is a barrier to better habits later; that is why the first formation of habits in early infancy is so important. If the first habits are good, endless trouble is saved later. Moreover habits acquired very early feel, in later life, just like instincts; they have the same profound grip. New contrary habits acquired afterwards cannot have the same force; for this reason, also, the first habits should be a matter of grave concern.

Two considerations come in when we are considering habit-formation in infancy. The first and paramount consideration is health; the second is character. We want the child to become the sort of person that will be liked and will be able to cope with life successfully. Fortunately, health and character point in the same direction: what is good for one is good also for the other. It is character that specially concerns us in this book; but health requires the same practices. Thus we are not faced with the difficult alternative of a healthy scoundrel or a diseased saint.

Every educated mother nowadays knows such simple facts as the importance of feeding the infant at regular intervals, not whenever it cries. This practice has arisen because it is better for the child's digestion, which is an entirely sufficient reason. But it is also desirable from the point of view of moral education. Infants are far more cunning than grown-up people are apt to suppose; if they find that crying produces agreeable results, they will cry. When, in later life, a habit of complaining causes them to be disliked instead of petted, they feel surprised and resentful, and the world seems to them cold and unsympathetic. If, however, they grow up into charming women, they will still be petted when they are querulous, and the bad training begun in childhood will be intensified. The same thing is true of rich men. Unless the right methods are adopted in infancy, people in later life will be either discontented or grasping, according to the degree of their power. The right moment to begin the requisite moral training is the moment of birth, because then it can be begun without disappointing expectations. At any later time it will have to fight against contrary habits, and will therefore be met by resentful indignation.

In dealing with the infant, therefore, there is need of a delicate balance between neglect and indulgence. Everything necessary for health must be done. The child must be picked up when it suffers from wind, it must be kept dry and warm. But if it cries when there is no adequate physical cause, it must be left to cry; if not, it will quickly develop into a tyrant. When it is attended to, there should not be too much fuss: what is necessary must be done, but without excessive expressions of sympathy. At no period of its life must it be regarded as an agreeable pet, somewhat more interesting than a lap-dog. It must from the very first be viewed seriously, as a potential adult. Habits which would be intolerable in an adult may be quite pleasant in a child. Of course the child cannot actually have the habits of an adult, but we should avoid everything that places an obstacle in the way of the acquisition of these habits. Above all, we should not give the child a sense of self-importance which later experience will mortify, and which, in any case, is not in accordance with the facts.

The difficulty in the education of young infants is largely the delicate balance required in the parent. Constant watchfulness and much labour are needed to avoid injury to health; these qualities will hardly exist in the necessary degree except where there is strong parental affection. But where this exists, it is very likely not to be wise. To the devoted parent, the child is immensely important. Unless care is taken, the child feels this, and judges himself as important as his parents feel him. In later life, his social environment will not regard him so fondly, and habits which assume that he is the centre of other people's universe will lead to disappointment. It is therefore necessary, not only in the first year, but afterwards also, that the parents should be breezy and cheerful and rather matter-of-fact where the child's possible ailments are concerned. In old days, infants were at once restricted and coddled: their limbs were not free, they were too warmly dressed, they were hampered in their spontaneous activities, but they were petted, sung to, rocked and dandled. This was ideally wrong, since it turned them into helpless pampered parasites.[1] The right rule is: encourage spontaneous activities, but discourage demands upon others. Do not let the child see how much you do for it, or how much trouble you take. Let it, wherever possible, taste the joy of a success achieved by its own efforts, not

[1] If it be objected that, after all, the world progressed, the reply is that it did not progress nearly as fast as it might have done, or as it will do if children are wisely handled.

extracted by tyrannizing over the grown-ups. Our aim, in modern education, is to reduce external discipline to a minimum; but this requires an internal self-discipline which is much more easily acquired in the first year of life than at any other time. For example: when you want a child to sleep, do not wheel it up and down, or take it in your arms, or even stay where it can see you. If you do this once, the child will demand that you should do it next time; in an incredibly short space of time it becomes a terrific business to get the child to sleep. Make it warm and dry and comfortable, put it down firmly, and after a few quiet remarks leave it to itself. It may cry for a few minutes, but unless it is ill it will soon stop. If you then go to look, you will find that it is fast asleep. And it will sleep far more with this treatment than with petting and indulgence.

The new-born infant, as we observed before, has no habits, but only reflexes and instincts. It follows that his world is not composed of "objects". Recurrent experiences are necessary for recognition, and recognition is necessary before the conception of an "object" can arise. The feel of the cot, the feel and smell of the mother's breast (or the bottle), and the mother's or nurse's voice will soon come to be familiar. The visual appearance of the mother or the cot comes somewhat later, because the new-born child does not know how to focus so as to see shapes distinctly. It is only gradually, through the formation of habits by association, that touch and sight and smell and hearing come together and coalesce in the common-sense notion of an object, of which one manifestation leads to the expectation of another. Even then, for a time, there is hardly any feeling of the difference between persons and things; a baby which is partly breast-fed and partly bottle-fed will, for a time, have similar feelings towards mother and bottle. During all this time, education must be by purely physical means. Its pleasures are physical—chiefly food and warmth—and its pains also are physical. Habits of behaviour arise through seeking what is associated with pleasure and avoiding what is associated with pain. A child's crying is partly a reflex connected with pain, partly an act performed in the pursuit of pleasure. At first, of course, it is only the former. But since any real pain that the child may be suffering must, if possible, be removed, it is inevitable that crying should come to be associated with pleasant consequences. The child therefore soon begins to cry because it desires a pleasure, not because it feels a physical pain; this is one of its first triumphs of intelligence. But try as it may, it cannot give quite

18

the same cry as when it is in actual pain. The attentive ear of the mother knows the difference, and if she is wise she will ignore the cry that is not an expression of physical pain. It is easy and agreeable to amuse an infant by dandling it or singing to it. But it learns with amazing rapidity to demand more and more of such amusements, which soon interfere with necessary sleep—and sleep ought to occupy almost all the day except meal-times. Some of these precepts may seem harsh, but experience shows that they make for the child's health and happiness.

But while the amusements which grown-up people provide should be kept within certain limits, those which the infant can enjoy for itself should be encouraged to the utmost. From the first, it should have opportunities to kick and practise its muscles. How our ancestors can have so long persisted in the practice of swaddling-clothes is almost inconceivable; it shows that even parental affection has difficulty in overcoming laziness, since the infant whose limbs are free needs more attention. As soon as the child can focus, it finds pleasure in watching moving objects, especially things that wave in the wind. But the number of possible amusements is small until the child has learned to grasp objects that it sees. Then, immediately, there is an enormous accession of pleasure. For some time, the exercise of grasping is enough to secure the happiness of many waking hours. Pleasure in a rattle also comes at this stage. Slightly earlier is the conquest of the toes and fingers. At first, the movement of the toes is purely reflex; then the baby discovers that they can be moved at will. This gives all the pleasure of an imperialist conquering a foreign country: the toes cease to be alien bodies and become incorporated in the ego. From this time onward, the child should be able to find many amusements, provided suitable objects are within his reach. And a child's amusements, for the most part, will be just what its education requires—provided, of course that it is not allowed to tumble, or to swallow pins, or otherwise injure itself.

The first three months of life are, on the whole, a somewhat dreary time for the infant, except during the moments when it is enjoying its meals. When it is comfortable, it sleeps; when it is awake, there is usually some discomfort. The happiness of a human being depends upon mental capacities, but these can find little outlet in an infant under three months, for lack of experience and muscular control. Young animals enjoy life much sooner, because they depend more upon instinct and less upon experience; but the things an infant can do by instinct are too few to provide more than a minimum of pleasure and interest. On the whole, the first three months involve a good deal of boredom. But the boredom is necessary if there is to be enough sleep; if much is done to amuse the child, it will not sleep enough.

At about the age of two to three months, the child learns to smile, and to have feelings about persons which are different from its feelings about things. At this age, a social relation between mother and child begins to be possible: the child can and does show pleasure at the sight of the mother, and develops responses which are not merely animal. Very soon a desire for praise and approval grows up; in my own boy, it was first shown unmistakably at the age of five months, when he succeeded, after many attempts, in lifting a somewhat heavy bell off the table, and ringing it while he looked round at everybody with a proud smile. From this moment, the educator has a new weapon: praise and blame. This weapon is extraordinarily powerful throughout childhood, but it must be used with great caution. There should not be any blame at all during the first year, and afterwards it should be used very sparingly. Praise is less harmful. But it should not be given so easily as to lose its value, nor should it be used to overstimulate a child. No tolerable parent could refrain from praising a child when it first walks and when it first says an intelligible word. And generally, when a child has mastered a difficulty after persistent efforts, praise is a proper reward. Moreover it is well to let the child feel that you sympathize with his desire to learn.

But on the whole an infant's desire to learn is so strong that parents need only provide opportunity. Give the child a chance to develop, and his own efforts will do the rest. It is not necessary to teach a child to crawl, or to walk, or to learn any of the other elements of muscular control. Of course we teach a child to talk by talking to it, but I doubt whether any purpose is served by deliberate attempts to teach words. Children learn at their own pace, and it is a mistake to try to force them. The great incentive to effort, all through life, is experience of success after initial difficulties. The difficulties must not be so great as to cause discouragement, or so small as not to stimulate effort. From birth to death, this is a fundamental principle. It is by what we do ourselves that we learn. What grown-up people can do is to perform some simple action that the child would like to perform, such as rattling a rattle, and then let the child find out how to do it. What others do is merely a stimulus to ambition; it is never in itself an education.

Regularity and routine are of the utmost importance in early childhood, and most of all in the first year of life. In regard to sleep, food, and evacuation, regular habits should be formed from the start. Moreover familiarity of surroundings is very important mentally. It teaches recognition, it avoids overstrain, and it produces a feeling of safety. I have sometimes thought that belief in the uniformity of nature, which is said to be a postulate of science, is entirely derived from the wish for safety. We can cope with the expected, but if the laws of nature were suddenly changed we should perish. The infant, because of its weakness, has need of reassurance, and it will be happier if everything that happens seems to happen according to invariable laws, so as to be predictable. In later childhood, the love of adventure develops, but in the first year of life everything unusual tends to be alarming. Do not let the child feel fear if you can possibly help it. If it is ill, and you are anxious, hide your anxiety very carefully, lest it should pass to the child by suggestion. Avoid everything that might produce excitement. And do not minister to the child's self-importance by letting it see that you mind if it does not sleep or eat or evacuate as it should. This applies not only to the first year of life, but still more to the subsequent years. Never let the child think that a necessary normal action, such as eating which ought to be a pleasure, is something that you desire, and that you want it to do so to please you. If you do, the child soon perceives that it has acquired a new source of power, and expects to be coaxed into actions which it ought to perform spontaneously. Do not imagine that the child has not the intelligence for such behaviour. Its powers are small and its knowledge is limited, but it has just as much intelligence as a grown-up person where these limitations do not operate. It learns more in the first twelve months than it will ever learn again in the same space of time, and this would be impossible if it had not a very active intelligence.

To sum up: Treat even the youngest baby with respect, as a person who will have to take his place in the world. Do not sacrifice his future to your present convenience, or to your pleasure in making much of him: the one is as harmful as the other. Here, as elsewhere, a combination of love and knowledge is necessary if the right way is to be followed.

In the following chapters, I propose to deal with various aspects of moral education, especially in the years ·from the second to the sixth. By the time the child is six years old, moral education ought to be nearly complete; that is to say, the further virtues which will be required in later years ought to be developed by the boy or girl spontaneously, as a result of good habits already existing and ambitions already stimulated. It is only where early moral training has been neglected or badly given that much will be needed at later ages.

I suppose that the child has reached the age of twelve months healthy and happy, with the foundations of a disciplined character already well laid by the methods considered in the preceding chapter. There will, of course, be some children whose health is bad, even if parents take all the precautions known to science at present. But we may hope that their number will be enormously diminished as time goes on. They ought, even now, to be so few as to be statistically unimportant, if existing knowledge were adequately applied. I do not propose to consider what ought to be done with children whose early training has been bad. This is a problem for the school-master, not for the parent; and it is especially to the parent that this book is addressed.

The second year of life should be one of great happiness. Walking and talking are new accomplishments, bringing a sense of freedom and power. Every day the child improves in both.[1] Independent play becomes possible, and the child has a more vivid sense of "seeing the world" than a man can derive from the most extensive globe-trotting. Birds and flowers, rivers and the sea, motor-cars and trains and steamers all bring delight and passionate interest. Curiosity is boundless: "want to see" is one of the commonest phrases at this age. Running freely in a garden or a field or on the seashore produces an ecstasy of emancipation after the confinement of crib and baby-carriage. Digestion is usually stronger than in the first year, food is more varied, and mastication is a new joy. For all these reasons, if the child is well cared for and healthy, life is a delicious adventure.

But with the greater independence of walk-

[1] This is perhaps not strictly accurate. Most children have periods of apparent stagnation, which cause anxiety to inexperienced parents. But probably throughout these periods there is progress in ways that are not easily perceptible.

ing and running there is apt to come also a new timidity. The new-born infant can easily be frightened; Dr. J. B. and Mrs. Watson found that the things which alarm it most are loud noises and the sensation of being dropped.[2] It is, however, so completely protected that it has little occasion for the rational exercise of fear; even in real dangers it is helpless, so that fear would not be of any use to it. During the second and third year, new fears develop. It is a moot point how far this is due to suggestion, and how far it is instinctive. The fact that the fears do not exist during the first year is not conclusive against their instinctive character, since an instinct may ripen at any age. Not even the most extreme Freudian would maintain that the sex-instinct is mature at birth. Obviously children who can run about by themselves have more need of fear than infants that cannot walk; it would therefore not be surprising if the instinct of fear arose with the need. The question is of considerable educational importance. If all fears arise from suggestion, they can be prevented by the simple expedient of not showing fear or aversion before a child. If, on the other hand, some of them are instinctive, more elaborate methods will be required.

Dr. Chalmers Mitchell, in his book "The

[2] "Studies in Infant Psychology", *Scientific Monthly,* December, 1921, p. 506.

Childhood of Animals", gives a large number of observations and experiments to show that there is usually no inherited instinct of fear in young animals.[3] Except monkeys and a few birds, they view the age-long enemies of their species, such as snakes, without the slightest alarm, unless their parents have taught them to feel fear of these animals. Children well under a year old seem never to be afraid of animals. Dr. Watson taught one such child to be afraid of rats by repeatedly sounding a gong behind its head at the moment when he showed it a rat. The noise was terrifying, and the rat came to be so by association. But instinctive fear of animals seems quite unknown in the early months. Fear of the dark, also, seems never to occur in children who have not been exposed to the suggestion that the dark is terrifying. There are certainly very strong grounds for the view that most of the fears which we used to regard as instinctive are acquired, and would not arise if grown-up people did not create them.

In order to get fresh light on this subject, I have observed my own children carefully; but as I could not always know what nurses and maids might have said to them, the interpretation of the facts was often doubtful. So far

[3] I came to know of these passages from a quotation in Dr. Paul Bousfield's "Sex and Civilization", where the same point of view is strongly advocated.

as I could judge, they bore out Dr. Watson's views as to fear in the first year of life. In the second year, they showed no fear of animals, except that one of them, for a time, was afraid of horses. This, however, was apparently due to the fact that a horse had suddenly galloped past her with a very loud noise. She is still in her second year, and therefore for later observation I am dependent on the boy. Near the end of his second year, he had a new nurse who was generally timid and especially afraid of the dark. He quickly acquired her terrors (of which we were ignorant at first); he fled from dogs and cats, cowered in abject fear before a dark cupboard,·wanted lights in every part of the room after dark, and was even afraid of his little sister the first time he saw her, thinking, apparently, that she was a strange animal of some unknown species.[4] All these fears might have been acquired from the timid nurse; in fact they gradually faded away after she was gone. There were other fears, however, which could not be accounted for in the same way, since they began before the nurse came, and were directed to objects which no grown-up person would find alarming. Chief of these was a fear of everything that moved in a surprising way, notably shadows and mechanical

[4] I think this fear was the same as the fear of mechanical toys. He saw her first asleep, and thought she was a doll; when she moved he was startled.

toys. After making this observation, I learned that fears of this sort are normal in childhood, and that there are strong reasons for regarding them as instinctive. The matter is discussed by William Stern in his "Psychology of Early Childhood", p. 494 ff, under the heading "Fear of the Mysterious". What he says is as follows:

The special significance of this form of fear, particularly in early childhood, has escaped the notice of the older school of child-psychologists; it has lately been established by Groos and by us. "Fear of the unaccustomed seems to be more a part of primitive nature than fear of a known danger" (Groos, p. 284). If the child meets with anything that does not fit in with the familiar course of his perception, three things are possible. Either the impression is so alien that it is simply rejected as a foreign body, and consciousness takes no notice of it. Or the interruption of the usual course of perception is pronounced enough to attract attention but not so violent as to effect disturbance; it is rather surprise, desire for knowledge, the beginning of all thought, judgment, enquiry. Or, lastly, the new suddenly breaks in upon the old with violent intensity, throws familiar ideas into unexpected confusion without a possibility of an immediate practical adjustment; then follows a shock with a strong affective-tone of displeasure, the fear of the mysterious (uncanny). Groos now has pointed out with keen insight that this fear of the uncanny is also distinctly founded on instinctive fear; it corresponds to a biological necessity which works from one generation to the next.

Stern gives many instances, among others fear of a suddenly opened umbrella and "the frequent fear of mechanical toys". The former, by the way, is very strong in horses and cows: a large herd can be driven into headlong flight by it, as I have verified. My own boy's terrors, under this head, were just such as Stern describes. The shadows that frightened him were vague quickly-moving shadows thrown into a room by unseen objects (such as omnibuses) passing in the street. I cured him by making shadows on the wall and the floor with my fingers, and getting him to imitate me; before long, he felt that he understood shadows and began to enjoy them. The same principle applied to mechanical toys: when he had seen the mechanism he was no longer frightened. But when the mechanism was invisible the process was slow. Some one gave him a cushion which emitted a long melancholy whine after being sat upon or pressed. This alarmed him for a long time. In no case did we entirely remove the terrifying object: we put it at a distance, where it was only slightly alarming; we produced gradual familiarity; and we persisted till the fear completely ceased. Generally the same mysterious quality which caused fear at first produced delight when the fear had been overcome. I think an irrational fear should never be simply let alone, but should be gradually overcome by familiarity with its fainter forms.

We adopted an exactly opposite process—perhaps wrongly—in the case of two rational fears which were wholly absent. I live half the year on a rocky coast where there are many precipices. The boy had no sense whatever of the danger of heights, and would have run straight over a cliff into the sea if we had let him. One day when we were sitting on a steep slope that ended in a sheer drop of a hundred feet, we explained to him quietly, as a merely scientific fact, that if he went over the edge he would fall and break like a plate. (He had lately seen a plate broken into many pieces by being dropped on the floor.) He sat still for some time, saying to himself "fall", "break", and then asked to be taken further from the edge. This was at the age of about two and a half. Since then he has had just enough fear of heights to make him safe while we keep an eye on him. But he would still be very rash if left to himself. He now (three and nine months) jumps from heights of six feet without hesitation, and would jump twenty feet if we would let him. Thus the instruction in apprehension certainly did not produce excessive results. I attribute this to the fact that it was instruction, not suggestion; neither of us was feeling fear when the instruction was given. I egard this as very important in education. Rational apprehension of dangers is necessary; fear is not. A child cannot apprehend dangers without *some* element of fear, but this element is very much diminished when it is not present in the instructor. A grown-up person in charge of a child should never feel fear. That is one reason why courage should be cultivated in women just as much as in men.

The second illustration was less deliberate. One day when I was walking with the boy (at the age of three years and four months) we found an adder on the path. He had seen pictures of snakes, but had never before seen a real snake. He did not know that snakes bite. He was delighted with the adder, and when it glided away he ran after it. As I knew he could not catch it, I did not check him, and did not tell him that snakes are dangerous. His nurse, however, from that time on, prevented him from running in long grass, on the ground that there might be snakes. A slight fear grew up in him as a result, but not more than we felt to be desirable.

The most difficult fear to overcome, so far, has been fear of the sea. Our first attempt to take the boy into the sea was at the age of two and a half. At first, it was quite impossible. He disliked the cold of the water, he was frightened by the noise of the waves, and they seemed to him to be always coming, never going. If the waves were big, he would not even go near to the sea. This was a period of general timidity; animals, odd noises, and various other things, caused alarm. We dealt with fear of the sea piecemeal. We put the boy into shallow pools away from the sea, until the mere cold had ceased to be a shock; at the end of the four warm months, he enjoyed paddling in shallow water at a distance from waves, but still cried if we put him into deep pools where the water came up to his waist. We accustomed him to the noise of the waves by letting him play for an hour at a time just out of sight of them; then we took him to where he could see them, and made him notice that after coming in they go out again. All this, combined with the example of his parents and other children, only brought him to the point where he could be *near* the waves without fear. I am convinced that the fear was instinctive; I am fairly certain there had **been** no suggestion to cause it. The following summer, at the age of three and a half, **we** took the matter up again. There was still **a** terror of going actually into the waves. After some unsuccessful coaxing, combined with the spectacle of everybody else bathing, we adopted old-fashioned methods. When he showed cowardice, we made him feel that we were ashamed of him; when he showed courage, we praised him warmly. Every day for about a fortnight, we plunged him up to the neck in the sea, in spite of his struggles and cries.[5] Every day hey grew less; before they ceased, he began to ask to be put in. At the end of a fortnight, the desired result had been achieved: he no longer feared the sea. From that moment, we left him completely free, and he bathed of his own accord whenever the weather was suitable —obviously with the greatest enjoyment. Fear had not ceased altogether, but had been partly repressed by pride. Familiarity, however, made the fear grow rapidly less, and it has now ceased altogether. His sister, now twenty months old, has never shown any fear of the sea, and runs straight in without the slightest hesitation.

I have related this matter in some detail, because, to a certain extent, it goes against modern theories for which I have much respect. The use of force in education should be very rare. But for the conquest of fear it is, I think, sometimes salutary. Where a fear is irrational and strong, the child, left to himself, will never have the experiences which show that there is no ground for apprehension. When a situation has been experienced repeatedly without harm,

[5] The method adopted with me at the same age was to pick me up by the heels and hold my head under water for some time. This method, oddly enough, succeeded in making me like the water; nevertheless I do not recommend it.

familiarity kills fear. It would very likely b
useless to give the dreaded experience *once*; i
must be given often enough to become in n
degree surprising. If the necessary experienc
can be secured without force, so much the bet
ter; but if not, force may be better than th
persistence of an unconquered fear.

There is a further point. In the case of m
own boy, and presumably in other cases too, th
experience of overcoming fear is extraordinar
ily delightful. It is easy to rouse the boy'
pride: when he has won praise for courage
he is radiantly happy for the rest of the day
At a later stage, a timid boy suffers agonie
through the contempt of other boys, and it i
much more difficult then for him to acquir
new habits. I think therefore that the earl
acquisition of self-control in the matter of fear
and the early teaching of physical enterprise
are of sufficient importance to warrant some
what drastic methods.

Parents learn by their mistakes; it is only
when the children are grown up that one dis
covers how they ought to have been educated
I shall therefore relate an incident which show
the snares of overindulgence. At the age o
two and a half, my boy was put to sleep in a
room by himself. He was inordinately prouc
of the promotion from the night-nursery, anc
at first he always slept quietly through the

36

ight. But one night there was a terrific gale, and a hurdle was blown over with a deafening crash. He woke in terror, and cried out. I went to him at once: he had apparently waked with a nightmare, and clung to me with his heart beating wildly. Very soon his terror ceased. But he had complained that it was dark—usually, at that time of year, he slept all through the dark hours. After I left him, the terror seemed to return in a mitigated form, so I gave him a night-light. After that, he made an almost nightly practice of crying out, until at last it became clear that he was only doing it for the pleasure of having grown-up people come and make a fuss. So we talked to him very carefully about the absence of danger in the dark, and told him that if he woke he was to turn over and go to sleep again, as we should not come to him unless there was something serious the matter. He listened attentively, and never cried out again except for grave cause on rare occasions. Of course the night-light was discontinued. If we had been more indulgent, we should probably have made him sleep badly for a long time, perhaps for life.

So much from personal experience. We must now pass on to a more general consideration of methods for eliminating fear.

After the first years, the proper instructors in .

physical courage are other children. If a chil
has older brothers and sisters, they will stimu
late it both by example and by precept, an
whatever they can do it will attempt. A
school, physical cowardice is despised, and ther
is no need for grown-up teachers to emphasiz
the matter. At least, that is the case amon;
boys. It ought to be equally the case amon;
girls, who should have precisely the sam
standards of courage. In physical ways, fortu
nately, school-girls are no longer taught to b
"lady-like", and their natural impulses toward
physical prowess are allowed a fair amount o:
scope. There is still, however, some differenc
between boys and girls in this respect. I an
convinced there ought to be none.[6]

When I speak of courage as desirable, I an
taking a purely behaviorist definition: a mar
is courageous when he does things which other:
might fail to do owing to fear. If he feels n
fear, so much the better; I do not regard contro
of fear by the will as the only true courage, o
even as the best form of courage. The secre
of modern moral education is to produce results by means of good habits which were formerly produced (or attempted) by self-contro
and will-power. Courage due to the will produces nervous disorders, of which "shell-
shock" afforded numerous instances. The fears

[6] See Bousfield, "Sex and Civilization", *passim*.

38

which had been repressed forced their way to the surface in ways not recognizable to introspection. I do not mean to suggest that self-control can be dispensed with entirely; on the contrary, no man can live a consistent life without it. What I do mean is, that self-control ought only to be needed in unforeseen situations, for which education has not provided in advance. It would have been foolish, even if it had been possible, to train the whole population to have, without effort, the sort of courage that was needed in the war. This was an exceptional and temporary need, of so extraordinary a kind that all other education would have had to be stunted if the habits required in the trenches had been instilled in youth.

The late Dr. Rivers, in his book on "Instinct and the Unconscious", gives the best psychological analysis of fear with which I am acquainted. He points out that one way of meeting a dangerous situation is manipulative activity, and that those who are able to employ this method adequately do not, at least consciously, feel the emotion of fear. It is a valuable experience, which stimulates both self-respect and effort, to pass gradually from fear to skill. Even so simple a matter as learning to ride a bicycle will give this experience in a mild form. In the modern world, owing to in-

crease of mechanism, this sort of skill is be
coming more and more important.

I suggest that training in physical courag
should be as far as possible given by teachin
skill in manipulating or controlling matter, nc
by means of bodily contests with other huma
beings. The kind of courage required fo
mountaineering, for manipulating an aeroplane
or for managing a small ship in a gale, seem
to me far more admirable than the sort re
quired in fighting. As far as possible, there
fore, I should train school-children in form
of more or less dangerous dexterity, rather tha
in such things as football. Where there is a
enemy to be overcome, let it be matter rathe
than other human beings. I do not mean tha
this principle should be applied pedantically
but that it should be allowed more weight in
athletics than is the case at present.

There are, of course, more passive aspects o
physical courage. There is endurance of hurt
without making a fuss; this can be taught t
children by not giving too much sympath
when they have small mishaps. A great deal o
hysteria in later life consists mainly of an exces
sive desire for sympathy: people invent ail
ments in the hope of being petted and treated
softly. This disposition can usually be pre
vented from developing by not encouraging
children to cry over every scratch and bruise

In this respect, the education of the nursery is still much worse for girls than for boys. It is just as bad to be soft with girls as with boys; if women are to be the equals of men, they must not be inferior in the sterner virtues.

I come now to the forms of courage that are not purely physical. These are the more important forms, but it is difficult to develop them adequately except on a foundation of the more elementary kinds.

The fear of the mysterious has been already touched upon, in connection with childish terrors. I believe this fear to be instinctive, and of immense historical importance. Most superstition is due to it. Eclipses, earthquakes, plagues, and such occurrences arouse it in a high degree among unscientific populations. It is a very dangerous form of fear, both individually and socially; to eradicate it in youth is therefore highly desirable. The proper antidote to it is scientific explanation. It is not necessary that everything which is mysterious at first sight should be explained: after a certain number of explanations have been given, the child will assume that there are explanations in other cases, and it will become possible to say that the explanation cannot be given yet. The important thing is to produce, as soon as possible, the feeling that the sense of mystery is only due to ignorance, which can be dispelled

41

by patience and mental effort. It is a remarkable fact that the very things which terrify children at first by their mysterious properties delight them as soon as fear is overcome. Thus mystery becomes an incentive to study, as soon as it ceases to promote superstition. My little boy, at the age of three and a half, spent many hours in absorbed solitary study of a garden syringe, until he had grasped how the water came in and the air came out, and how the converse process occurred. Eclipses can be explained so as to be intelligible even to very tiny children. Whatever either terrifies or interests the child should be explained if it is at all possible; this transforms fear into scientific interest by a process which is entirely along the lines of instinct and repeats the history of the race.

Some problems, in this connection, are difficult, and require much tact. The most difficult is death. The child soon discovers that plants and animals die. The chances are that somebody he knows will die before he is six years old. If he has at all an active mind, it occurs to him that his parents will die, and even that he will die himself. (This is more difficult to imagine.) These thoughts will produce a crop of questions, which must be answered carefully. A person whose beliefs are orthodox will have less difficulty than a person who thinks that there is no life after death. If you hold the latter view, do not say anything contrary to it; no consideration on earth justifies a parent in telling lies to his child. It is best to explain that death is a sleep from which people do not wake. This should be said without solemnity, as if it were the most ordinary thing imaginable. If the child worries about dying himself, tell him it is not likely to happen for many, many years. It would be useless, in early years, to attempt to instil a Stoic contempt for death. Do not introduce the topic, but do not avoid it when the child introduces it. Do all you can to make the child feel that there is no mystery about it. If he is a normal healthy child, these methods will suffice to keep him from brooding. At all ages, be willing to talk fully and frankly, to tell all that you believe, and to convey the impression that the subject is rather uninteresting. It is not good either for old or young to spend much time in thinking about death.

Apart from special fears, children are liable to a diffused anxiety. This is generally due to too much repression by their elders, and is therefore much less common than it used to be. Perpetual nagging, prohibition of noise, constant instruction in manners, used to make childhood a period of misery. I can remember, at the age of five, being told that childhood was the happiest period of life (a blank lie, in those days). I wept inconsolably, wished I were dead, and wondered how I should endure the boredom of the years to come. It is almost inconceivable, nowadays, that any one should say such a thing to a child. The child's life is instinctively prospective: it is always directed towards the things that will become possible later on. This is part of the stimulus to the child's efforts. To make the child retrospective, to represent the future as worse than the past, is to sap the life of the child at its source. Yet that is what heartless sentimentalists used to do by talking to the child about the joys of childhood. Fortunately the impression of their words did not last long. At most times, I believed the grown-ups must be perfectly happy, because they had no lessons and they could eat what they liked. This belief was healthy and stimulating.

Shyness is a distressing form of timidity, which is common in England and China, and parts of America, but rare elsewhere. It arises partly from having little to do with strangers, partly from insistence upon company manners. As far as is convenient, children should, after the first year, become accustomed to seeing strangers and being handled by them. As regards manners, they should, at first, be taught the bare minimum required for not being an intolerable nuisance.

It is better to let them see strangers for a few minutes without restraint and then be taken away, than to expect them to stay in the room and be quiet. But after the first two years it is a good plan to teach them to amuse themselves quietly part of the day, with pictures or clay or Montessori apparatus or something of the kind. There should always be a reason for quiet that they can understand. Manners should not be taught in the abstract, except when it can be done as an amusing game. But as soon as the child can understand he should realize that parents also have their rights; he must accord freedom to others, and have freedom for himself to the utmost possible extent. Children easily appreciate justice, and will readily accord to others what others accord to them. This is the core of good manners.

Above all, if you wish to dispel fear in your children, be fearless yourself. If you are afraid of thunderstorms, the child will catch your fear the first time he hears thunder in your presence. If you express a dread of social revolution, the child will feel a fright all the greater for not knowing what you are talking about. If you are apprehensive about illness, so will your child be. Life is full of perils, but the wise man ignores those that are inevitable, and acts prudently but without emotion as regards those that can be avoided. You cannot avoid dying, but you can avoid dying intestate; therefore make your will, and forget that you are mortal. Rational provision against misfortune is a totally different thing from fear; it is a part of wisdom, whereas all fear is slavish. If you cannot avoid feeling fears, try to prevent your child from suspecting them. Above all, give him that wide outlook and that multiplicity of vivid interests that will prevent him, in later life, from brooding upon possibilities of personal misfortune. Only so can you make him a free citizen of the universe.

PLAY AND FANCY

LOVE of play is the most obvious distinguishing mark of young animals, whether human or otherwise. In human children, this is accompanied by an inexhaustible pleasure in pretence. Play and pretence are a vital need of childhood, for which opportunity must be provided if the child is to be happy and healthy, quite independently of any further utility in these activities. There are two questions which concern education in this connection: first, what should parents and schools do in the way of providing opportunity? and secondly, should they do anything more, with a view to increasing the educational usefulness of games?

Let us begin with a few words about the psychology of games. This has been exhaustively treated by Groos; a shorter discussion will be found in William Stern's book mentioned in the preceding chapter. There are two separate questions in this matter: the first is as to the impulses which produce play, the second is as to its biological utility. The second is the easier question. There seems no reason to doubt the most widely accepted theory, that in play the young of any species rehearse and practise the activities which they will have to perform in earnest later on. The play of puppies is exactly like a dog-fight, except that they do not actually bite each other. The play of kittens resembles the behaviour of cats with mice. Children love to imitate any work they have been watching, such as building or digging; the more important the work seems to them, the more they like to play at it. And they enjoy anything that gives them new muscular facilities, such as jumping, climbing, or walking up a narrow plank—always provided the task is not too difficult. But although this accounts, in a general way, for the usefulness of the play-impulse, it does not by any means cover all its manifestations, and must not for a moment be regarded as giving a psychological analysis.

Some psycho-analysts have tried to see a sexual symbolism in children's play. This, I am convinced, is utter moonshine. The main instinctive urge of childhood is not sex, but the desire to become adult, or, perhaps more correctly, the will to power.[1] The child is impressed by his own weakness in comparison with

[1] Cf. "The Nervous Child" by Dr. H. C. Cameron (3rd ed., Oxford, 1924), p. 32 ff.

older people, and he wishes to become their equal. I remember my boy's profound delight when he realized that he would one day be a man and that I had once been a child; one could see effort being stimulated by the realization that success was possible. From a very early age, the child wishes to do what older people do, as is shown by the practice of imitation. Older brothers and sisters are useful, because their purposes can be understood and their capacities are not so far out of reach as those of grown-up people. The feeling of inferiority is very strong in children; when they are normal and rightly educated, it is a stimulus to effort, but if they are repressed it may become a source of unhappiness.

In play, we have two forms of the will to power: the form which consists in learning to do things, and the form which consists in fantasy. Just as the balked adult may indulge in daydreams that have a sexual significance, so the normal child indulges in pretences that have a power-significance. He likes to be a giant, or a lion, or a train; in his make-believe, he inspires terror. When I told my boy the story of Jack the Giant-Killer, I tried to make him identify himself with Jack, but he firmly chose the giant. When his mother told him the story of Bluebeard, he insisted on being Bluebeard, and regarded the wife as justly punished for insubordination. In his play, there was a sanguinary outbreak of cutting off ladies' heads. Sadism, Freudians would say; but he enjoyed just as much being a giant who ate little boys, or an engine that could pull a heavy load. Power, not sex, was the common element in these pretences. One day, when we were returning from a walk, I told him, as an obvious joke, that perhaps we should find a certain Mr. Tiddliewinks in possession of our house, and he might refuse to let us in. After that, for a long time, he would stand on the porch being Mr. Tiddliewinks, and telling me to go to another house. His delight in this game was unbounded, and obviously the pretence of power was what he enjoyed.

It would, however, be an undue simplification to suppose that the will to power is the sole source of children's play. They enjoy the pretence of terror—perhaps because the knowledge that it is a pretence increases their sense of safety. Sometimes I pretend to be a crocodile coming to eat my boy up. He squeals so realistically that I stop, thinking he is really frightened; but the moment I stop he says, "Daddy be a crocodile again". A good deal of the pleasure of pretence is sheer joy in drama— the same thing that makes adults like novels and the theatre. I think curiosity has a part in all this: by playing bears, the child feels as if he were getting to know about bears. I think every strong impulse in the child's life is reflected in play: power is only dominant in his play in proportion as it is dominant in his desires.

As regards the educational value of play, everybody would agree in praising the sort that consists in acquiring new aptitudes, but many moderns look with suspicion upon the sort that consists in pretence. Daydreams, in adult life, are recognized as more or less pathological, and as a substitute for efforts in the sphere of reality. Some of the discredit which has fallen upon daydreams has spilled over on to children's pretences, quite mistakenly, as I think. Montessori teachers do not like children to turn their apparatus into trains or steamers or what not: this is called "disordered imagination". They are quite right, because what the children are doing is not really play, even if to themselves it may seem to be nothing more. The apparatus amuses the child, but its purpose is instruction; the amusement is merely a means to instruction. In real play, amusement is the governing purpose. When the objection to "disordered imagination" is carried over into genuine play, it seems to me to go too far. The same thing applies to the objection to telling children about fairies and giants and witches and magic carpets and so on. I cannot sympathize with the ascetics of truth, any more than with ascetics of other kinds. It is commonly said that children do not distinguish between pretence and reality, but I see very little reason to believe this. We do not believe that Hamlet ever existed, but we should be annoyed by a man who kept reminding us of this while we were enjoying the play. So children are annoyed by a tactless reminder of reality, but are not in the least taken in by their own make-believe.

Truth is important, and imagination is important; but imagination develops earlier in the history of the individual, as in that of the race. So long as the child's physical needs are attended to, he finds games far more interesting than reality. In games he is a king: indeed he rules his territory with a power surpassing that of any mere earthly monarch. In reality he has to go to bed at a certain time, and to obey a host of tiresome precepts. He is exasperated when unimaginative adults interfere thoughtlessly with his *mise-en-scène*. When he has built a wall that not even the biggest giants can scale, and you carelessly step over it, he is as angry as Romulus was with Remus. Seeing that his inferiority to other people is normal, not pathological, its compensation in fantasy is also normal and not pathological. His games do not take up time which might be more profitably spent in other ways: if all his hours were given over to serious pursuits, he would soon become a nervous wreck. An adult who indulges in dreams may be told to exert himself in order to realize them; but a child cannot yet realize dreams which it is right that he should have. He does not regard his fancies as a permanent substitute for reality; on the contrary, he ardently hopes to translate them into fact when the time comes.

It is a dangerous error to confound truth with matter-of-fact. Our life is governed not only by facts, but by hopes; the kind of truthfulness which sees nothing but facts is a prison for the human spirit. Dreams are only to be condemned when they are a lazy substitute for an effort to change reality; when they are an incentive, they are fulfilling a vital purpose in the incarnation of human ideals. To kill fancy in childhood is to make a slave to what exists, a creature tethered to earth and therefore unable to create heaven.

This is all very well, you may say, but what has it to do with giants eating children, or Bluebeard cutting off his wives' heads? Are these things to exist in your heaven? Must not imagination be purified and ennobled before it can serve any good purpose? How can you, a pacifist, allow your innocent boy to revel in the thought of destroying human life? How can you justify a pleasure derived from instincts of savagery which the human race must outgrow? All this I imagine the reader has been feeling. The matter is important, and I will try to state why I hold to a different point of view.

Education consists in the cultivation of instincts, not in their suppression. Human instincts are very vague, and can be satisfied in a great variety of ways. Most of them require, for their gratification, some kind of skill. Cricket and baseball satisfy the same instinct, but a boy will play whichever he has learnt. Thus the secret of instruction, in so far as it bears upon character, is to give a man such kinds of skill as shall lead to his employing his instincts usefully. The instinct of power, which in the child is crudely satisfied by identification with Bluebeard, can find in later life a refined satisfaction by scientific discovery, or artistic creation, or the creation and education of splendid children, or any one of a thousand useful activities. If the only thing a man knows is how to fight, his will to power will make him delight in battle. But if he has other kinds of skill, he will find his satisfaction in other ways. If, however, his will to power has been nipped in the bud when he was a child, he will be listless and lazy, doing little good and little harm; he will be *"a Dio spiacente ed a' nemici sui."* This kind of milksop goodness is not what the world needs, or what we should try to produce collective play, as soon as it becomes possible, is so much more delightful that pleasure in playing alone quickly ceases. English upper-class education has always attributed an enormous moral importance to school games. To my mind, there is some exaggeration in the conventional British view, although I admit that games have certain important merits. They are good for health, provided they are not too expert; if exceptional skill is too much prized the best players overdo it, while the others tend to lapse into spectators. They teach boys and girls to endure hurts without making a fuss, and to incur great fatigue cheerfully. But the other advantages which are claimed for them seem to me largely illusory. They are said to teach co-operation, but in fact they only teach it in its competitive form. This is the form required in war, not in industry or in the right kind of social relations. Science has made it technically possible to substitute co-operation for competition, both in economics and in international politics; at the same time it has made competition (in the form of war) much more dangerous than it used to be. For these reasons, it is more important than in former times to cultivate the idea of co-operative enterprises in which the "enemy" is physical nature, rather than competitive enterprises in which there are human victors and vanquished. I do not want in our children. While they are small and cannot do much harm, it is biologically natural that they should, in imagination, live through the life of remote savage ancestors. Do not be afraid that they will remain at that level, if you put in their way the knowledge and skill required for more refined satisfactions. When I was a child, I loved to turn head over heels. I never do so now, though I should not think it wicked to do so. Similarly the child who enjoys being Bluebeard will outgrow this taste, and learn to seek power in other ways. And if his imagination has been kept alive in childhood by the stimuli appropriate to that stage, it is much more likely to remain alive in later years, when it can exercise itself in the ways suitable to a man. It is useless to obtrude moral ideas at an age at which they can evoke no response, and at which they are not yet required for the control of behaviour. The only effect is boredom, and imperviousness to those same ideas at the later age when they might have become potent. That is one reason, among others, why the study of child-psychology is of such vital importance to education.

The games of later years differ from those of early childhood by the fact that they become increasingly competitive. At first, a child's play is solitary; it is difficult for an infant to join in the games of older brothers and sisters. But to lay too much stress upon this consideration, because competitiveness is natural to man and must find some outlet, which can hardly be more innocent than games and athletic contests. This is a valid reason for not preventing games, but it is not a valid reason for exalting them into a leading position in the school curriculum. Let boys play because they like to do so, not because the authorities think games an antidote to what the Japanese call "dangerous thoughts".

I have said a great deal in an earlier chapter about the importance of overcoming fear and producing courage; but courage must not be confounded with brutality. Brutality is pleasure in forcing one's will upon other people; courage is indifference to personal misfortunes. I would teach boys and girls, if opportunity offered, to sail small ships in stormy seas, to dive from heights, to drive a motor-car or even an aeroplane. I would teach them, as Sanderson of Oundle did, to build machines and incur risks in scientific experiment. As far as possible, I would represent inanimate nature as the antagonist in the game; the will to power can find satisfaction in this contest just as well as in competing with other human beings. The skill acquired in this way is more useful than skill in cricket or football, and the character developed is more in accordance with social morality. And apart from moral qualities, the cult of athletics involves an under-estimation of intelligence. Great Britain is losing her industrial position, and will perhaps lose her empire, through stupidity, and through the fact that the authorities do not value or promote intelligence. All this is connected with the fanatical belief in the paramount importance of games. Of course it goes deeper: the belief that a young man's athletic record is a test of his worth is a symptom of our general failure to grasp the need of knowledge and thought in mastering the complex modern world. But on this topic I will say no more now, as it will be considered again at a later stage.

There is another aspect of school games, which is usually considered good but which I think on the whole bad; I mean, their efficacy in promoting *esprit de corps*. *Esprit de corps* is liked by authorities, because it enables them to utilize bad motives for what are considered to be good actions. If efforts are to be made they are easily stimulated by promoting the desire to surpass some other group. The difficulty is that no motive is provided for efforts which are not competitive. It is amazing how deeply the competitive motive has eaten into all our activities. If you wish to persuade a borough to improve the public provision for the care of children, you have to point out that some neighbouring borough has a lower infant mortality. If you wish to persuade a manufacturer to adopt a new process which is clearly an improvement, you have to emphasize the danger of competition. If you wish to persuade the War Office that a modicum of military knowledge is desirable in the higher commands—but no, not even fear of defeat will prevail in this case, so strong is the "gentlemanly" tradition.[2] Nothing is done to promote constructiveness for its own sake, or to make people take an interest in doing their job efficiently even if no one is to be injured thereby. Our economic system has more to do with this than school games. But school games, as they now exist, embody the spirit of competition. If the spirit of co-operation is to take its place, a change in school games will be necessary. But to develop this subject would take us too far from our theme. I am not considering the building of the good State, but the building of the good individual, in so far as this is possible in the existing State. Improvement in the individual and improvement in the community must go hand in hand, but it is the individual that specially concerns the writer on education.

[2] See *e.g.* "The Secret Corps", by Captain Ferdinand Tuohy, Chap. VI, (Murray, 1920).

CONSTRUCTIVENESS

THE subject of this chapter is one which has already been considered incidentally in connection with play, but it is now to be considered on its own account.

The instinctive desires of children, as we have seen, are vague; education and opportunity can turn them into many different channels. Neither the old belief in original sin, nor Rousseau's belief in natural virtue, is in accordance with the facts. The raw material of instinct is ethically neutral, and can be shaped either to good or evil by the influence of the environment. There is ground for a sober optimism in the fact that, apart from pathological cases, most people's instincts are, at first, capable of being developed into good forms; and the pathological cases would be very few, given proper mental and physical hygiene in the early years. A proper education would make it possible to live in accordance with instinct, but it would be a trained and cultivated instinct, not the crude unformed impulse which

is all that nature provides. The great culti-
vator of instinct is skill: skill which provides
certain kinds of satisfaction, but not others.
Give a man the right kinds of skill, and he will
be virtuous; give him the wrong kinds, or none
at all, and he will be wicked.

These general considerations apply with
special force to the will to power. We all like
to effect *something*, but so far as the love of
power is concerned we do not care what we
effect. Broadly speaking, the more difficult
the achievement the more it pleases us. Men
like fly-fishing, because it is difficult; they will
not shoot a bird sitting, because it is easy. I
take these illustrations, because in them a man
has no ulterior motive beyond the pleasure of
the activity. But the same principle applies
everywhere. I liked arithmetic until I learnt
Euclid, Euclid until I learnt analytical geom-
etry, and so on. A child, at first, delights in
walking, then in running, then in jumping
and climbing. What we can do easily no longer
gives us a sense of power; it is the newly-
acquired skill, or the skill about which we are
doubtful, that gives us the thrill of success.
That is why the will to power is so immeasur-
ably adaptable according to the type of skill
which is taught.

Construction and destruction alike satisfy
the will to power, but construction is more diffi-

cult as a rule, and therefore gives more satis-
tion to the person who can achieve it. I shall
not attempt to give a pedantically exact definition of construction and destruction; I suppose,
roughly speaking, we construct when we increase the potential energy of the system in
which we are interested, and we destroy when
we diminish its potential energy. Or, in more
psychological terms, we construct when we
produce a predesigned structure, and we destroy when we liberate natural forces to alter
an existing structure, without being interested
in the resulting new structure. Whatever may
be thought of these definitions, we all know in
practice whether an activity is to be regarded as
constructive or destructive, except in a few
cases where a man professes to be destroying
with a view to rebuilding and we are not sure
whether he is sincere.

Destruction being easier, a child's games
usually begin with it, and only pass on to construction at a later stage. A child on the sand
with a pail likes grown-up people to make sand-
puddings, and then knock them down with his
spade. But as soon as he can make sand-pud-
dings himself, he delights in doing so, and will
not permit them to be knocked down. When a
child first has bricks, he likes to destroy towers
built by his elders. But when he has learnt to
build for himself, he becomes inordinately

proud of his performances, and cannot bear to see his architectural efforts reduced to a heap of ruins. The impulse which makes the child enjoy the game is exactly the same at both stages, but new skill has changed the activity resulting from the impulse.

The first beginnings of many virtues arise out of experiencing the joys of construction. When a child begs you to leave his constructions undestroyed, you can easily make him understand that he must not destroy other people's. In this way you can create respect for the produce of labour, the only socially innocuous source of private property. You also give the child an incentive to patience, persistence, and observation; without these qualities, he will not succeed in building his tower to the height upon which he had set his heart. In play with children, you should only construct yourself sufficiently to stimulate ambition and to show how the thing is done; after that, construction should be left to their own efforts.

If a child has access to a garden, it is easy to cultivate a more elaborate form of constructiveness. The first impulse of a child in a garden is to pick every attractive flower. It is easy to check this by prohibition, but mere prohibition is inadequate as an education. One wants to produce in the child the same respect for the garden that restrains the grown-ups from picking wantonly. The respect of the grown-up is due to realization of the labour and effort required to produce the pleasing result. By the time a child is three years old, he can be given a corner of the garden and encouraged to plant seeds in it. When they come up and blossom, his own flowers seem precious and wonderful; then he can appreciate that his mother's flowers also must be treated with care.

The elimination of thoughtless cruelty is to be effected most easily by developing an interest in construction and growth. Almost every child, as soon as he is old enough, wants to kill flies and other insects; this leads on to the killing of larger animals, and ultimately of men. In the ordinary English upper-class family, the killing of birds is considered highly creditable, and the killing of men in war is regarded as the noblest of professions. This attitude is in accordance with untrained instinct: it is that of men who possess no form of constructive skill, and are therefore unable to find any innocent embodiment of their will to power. They can make pheasants die and tenants suffer; when occasion arises, they can shoot a rhinoceros or a German. But in more useful arts they are entirely deficient, as their parents and teachers thought it sufficient to make them into English gentlemen. I do not believe that at birth they are any stupider than other babies; their deficiencies in later life are entirely attributable to bad education. If, from an early age, they had been led to feel the value of life by watching its development with affectionate proprietorship; if they had acquired forms of constructive skill; if they had been made to realize with apprehension how quickly and easily a slow product of anxious solicitude can be destroyed —if all this had formed part of their early moral training, they would not be so ready to destroy what others have similarly created or tended. The great educator in this respect in later life is parenthood, provided the instinct is adequately aroused. But in the rich this seldom happens, because they leave the care of their children to paid professionals; therefore we cannot wait till they become parents before beginning to eradicate their destructive tendencies.

Every author who has had uneducated housemaids knows that it is difficult (the public may wish it were impossible) to restrain their passion for lighting the fire with his manuscripts. A fellow-author, even if he were a jealous enemy, would not think of doing such a thing, because experience has taught him the value of manuscripts. Similarly the boy who has a garden will not trample on other people's flower-beds, and the boy who has pets can be taught to respect animal life. Respect for human life is likely to exist in any one who has taken trouble over his or her own children. It is the trouble we take over our children that elicits the stronger forms of parental affection; in those who avoid this trouble the parental instinct becomes more or less atrophied, and remains only as a sense of responsibility. But parents are far more likely to take trouble over their children if their own constructive impulses have been fully developed; thus for this reason also it is very desirable to pay attention to this aspect of education.

When I speak of constructiveness, I am not thinking only of material construction. Such occupations as acting and choral singing involve co-operative non-material construction; they are pleasant to many children and young people, and should be encouraged (though not enforced). Even in purely intellectual matters it is possible to have a constructive or a destructive bias. A classical education is almost entirely critical: a boy learns to avoid mistakes, and to despise those who commit them. This tends to produce a kind of cold correctness, in which originality is replaced by respect for authority. Correct Latin is fixed once for all: it is that of Vergil and Cicero. Correct science is continually changing, and an able youth may look forward to helping in this process. Consequently the attitude produced by a scientific education is likely to be more constructive than that produced by the study of dead languages. Wherever avoidance of error is the chief thing aimed at, education tends to produce an intellectually bloodless type. The prospect of doing something venturesome with one's knowledge ought to be held before all the abler young men and young women. Too often, higher education is regarded as conferring something analogous to good manners, a merely negative code by which solecisms are avoided. In such an education, constructiveness has been forgotten. The usual type produced is, as might be expected, niggling, unenterprising, and lacking in generosity. All this is avoided when positive achievement is made the goal of education.

In the later years of education, there should be a stimulation of social constructiveness. I mean, that those whose intelligence is adequate should be encouraged in using their imaginations to think out more productive ways of utilizing existing social forces or creating new ones. Men read Plato's "Republic", but they do not attach it to current politics at any point. When I stated that the Russian State in 1920 had ideals which were almost exactly those of the "Republic", it was hard to say whether the Platonists or the Bolsheviks were the more shocked. People read a literary classic without any attempt to see what it means in terms of the lives of Brown, Jones and Robinson. This is particularly easy with a Utopia, because we are not told of any road which leads to it from our present social system. The valuable faculty, in these matters, is that of judging rightly as to the next step. British nineteenth-century Liberals had this merit, though the ultimate results to which their measures were bound to lead would have horrified them. A great deal depends upon the kind of image that dominates a man's thinking, often quite unconsciously. A social system may be conceived in many ways; the commonest are a mould, a machine, and a tree. The first belongs to the static conceptions of society, such as those of Sparta and traditional China: human nature is to be poured into a prepared mould, and to set in a preconceived shape. Something of this idea exists in any rigid moral or social convention. The man whose outlook is dominated by this image will have a political outlook of a certain kind—stiff and unyielding, stern and persecuting. The man who conceives of society as a machine is more modern. The industrialist and the communist alike belong to this class. To them, human nature is uninteresting, and the ends of life are simple—usually the maximizing of production. The purpose of social organization is to secure these simple ends. The difficulty is hat actual human beings will not desire them; hey persist in wanting all kinds of chaotic hings which seem worthless to the tidy mind of the organizer. This drives the organizer back to the mould, in order to produce human beings who desire what he thinks good. And his, in turn, leads to revolution.

The man who imagines a social system as a ree will have a different political outlook. A bad machine can be scrapped, and another put in its place. But if a tree is cut down, it is a long time before a new tree achieves the same strength and size. A machine or a mould is what its maker chooses; a tree has its specific nature, and can only be made into a better or worse example of the species. Constructiveness applied to living things is quite different from constructiveness applied to machines; it has humbler functions, and requires a sort of sympathy. For that reason, in teaching constructiveness to the young, they should have opportunities of exercising it upon plants and animals, not only upon bricks and machines. Physics has been dominant in thought since the time of Newton, and in practice since the industrial revolution; this has brought with it a rather mechanical conception of society. Biological evolution introduced a new set of ideas, but they were somewhat overshadowed by natural selection, which it should be our aim to eliminate from human affairs by eugenics, birth-control, and education. The conception of society as a tree is better than the mould or the machine, but it is still defective. It is to psychology that we must look to supply the deficiency. Psychological constructiveness is a new and special kind, very little understood as yet. It is essential to a right theory of education, politics, and all purely human affairs. And it should dominate the imaginations of citizens, if they are not to be misled by false analogies. Some people dread constructiveness in human affairs, because they fear that it must be mechanical; they therefore believe in anarchism and the "return to nature". I am trying in this book to show, in concrete instances, how psychological construction differs from the construction of a machine. The imaginative side of this idea ought to be made familiar in higher education; if it were, I believe that our politics would cease to be angular and sharp and destructive, becoming instead supple and truly scientific, with the development of splendid men and women as its goal.

SELFISHNESS AND PROPERTY

I COME now to a problem analogous to that of Fear, in that we are concerned with an impulse which is strong, partly instinctive, and largely undesirable. In all such cases, we have to be careful not to thwart a child's nature. It is useless to shut our eyes to his nature, or to wish that it were different; we must accept the raw material which is provided, and not attempt to treat it in ways only applicable to some different material.

Selfishness is not an ultimate ethical conception; the more it is analysed, the vaguer it becomes. But as a phenomenon in the nursery it is perfectly definite, and presents problems with which it is very necessary to cope. Left to himself, an older child will seize a younger child's toys, demand more than his share of grown-up attention, and generally pursue his desires regardless of the younger child's disappointments. A human ego, like a gas, will always expand unless restrained by external pressure. The object of education, in this respect, is to let the external pressure take the form of habits, ideas and sympathies in the child's own mind, not of knocks and blows and punishments. The idea which is needed is that of justice, not self-sacrifice. Every person has a right to a certain amount of room in the world, and should not be made to feel wicked in standing up for what is due to him. When self-sacrifice is taught, the idea seems to be that it will not be fully practised, and that the practical result will be about right. But in fact people either fail to learn the lesson, or feel sinful when they demand mere justice, or carry self-sacrifice to ridiculous extremes. In the last case, they feel an obscure resentment against the people to whom they make renunciations, and probably allow selfishness to return by the back door of a demand for gratitude. In any case, self-sacrifice cannot be true doctrine, because it cannot be universal; and it is most undesirable to teach falsehood as a means to virtue, because when the falsehood is perceived the virtue evaporates. Justice, on the contrary, can be universal. Therefore justice is the conception that we ought to try to instil into the child's thoughts and habits.

It is difficult, if not impossible, to teach justice to a solitary child. The rights and desires of grown-up people are so different from those of children that they make no imaginative appeal; there is hardly ever direct competition for exactly the same pleasure. Moreover, as the grown-up people are in a position to exact obedience to their own demands, they have to be judges in their own case, and do not produce upon the child the effect of an impartial tribunal. They can, of course, give definite precepts inculcating this or that form of convenient behaviour: not to interrupt when their mother is counting the wash, not to shout when their father is busy, not to obtrude their concerns when there are visitors. But these are inexplicable requirements, to which, it is true, the child submits willingly enough if otherwise kindly treated, but which make no appeal to his own sense of what is reasonable. It is right that the child should be made to obey such rules, because he must not be allowed to be a tyrant, and because he must understand that other people attach importance to their own pursuits, however odd those pursuits may be. But not much more than external good behaviour is to be got by such methods; the real education in justice can only come where there are other children. This is one of many reasons why no child should long be solitary. Parents who have the misfortune to have an only child should do all that they can to secure companionship for it, even at the cost of a good deal of separation from home, if no other way is possible. A solitary child must be either suppressed or selfish—perhaps both by turns. A well-behaved only child is pathetic, and an ill-behaved one is a nuisance. In these days of small families, this is a more serious trouble than it used to be. It is one of the grounds for advocating nursery-schools, as to which I shall have more to say in a later chapter. But for the moment I shall assume a family of two at least, not very widely separated in age, so that their tastes are largely the same.

Where there is competition for a pleasure which can only be enjoyed by one at a time, such as a ride in a wheelbarrow, it will be found that the children readily understand justice. Their impulse, of course, is to demand the pleasure for themselves to the exclusion of the others, but it is surprising how quickly this impulse is overcome when the grown-ups institute the system of a turn for each. I do not believe that a sense of justice is innate, but I have been astonished to see how quickly it can be created. Of course, it must be real justice; there must not be any secret bias. If you are fonder of some of the children than of others, you must be on your guard to prevent your affections from having any influence on your distribution of pleasures. It is of course a generally recognized principle that toys must be equal.

It is quite useless to attempt to suppress the

demand for justice by any kind of moral training. Do not give more than justice, but do not expect the child to accept less. There is a chapter in "The Fairchild Family" on "The Secret Sins of the Heart" which illustrates the methods to be avoided. Lucy has maintained that she has been good, so her mother tells her that even when her behaviour is all right her thoughts are wrong, and quotes: "The heart is deceitful above all things and desperately wicked" (Jeremiah, xvii, 9). So Mrs. Fairchild gives Lucy a little book in which to record the "desperately wicked" things that are in her heart when outwardly she is good. At breakfast, her parents give a ribbon to her sister and a cherry to her brother, but nothing to her. She records in her book that at this point she had a very wicked thought, that her parents loved her brother and sister better than they loved her. She had been taught, and she believed, that she ought to cope with this thought by moral discipline; but by this method it could only be driven underground, to produce strange distorted effects in later years. The proper course would have been for her to express her feeling, and for her parents to dispel it either by giving her a present, too, or by explaining, in a way she could understand, that she must wait for another time, as no further present was available at the moment. Truth and frankness dispel difficulties, but the attempt at repressive moral discipline only aggravates them.

Closely connected with justice is the sense of property. This is a difficult matter, which must be dealt with by adaptable tact, not by any rigid set of rules. There are, in fact, conflicting considerations, which make it difficult to take a clear line. On the one hand, the love of property produces many terrible evils in later years; the fear of losing valued material possessions is one of the main sources of political and economic cruelty. It is desirable that men and women should, as far as possible, find their happiness in ways which are not subject to private ownership, *i.e.*, in creative rather than defensive activities. For this reason, it is unwise to cultivate the sense of property in children if it can be helped. But before proceeding to act upon this view, there are some very strong arguments on the other side, which it would be dangerous to neglect. In the first place, the sense of property is very strong in children; it develops as soon as they can grasp objects which they see (the hand-eye co-ordination). What they grasp, they feel is theirs, and they are indignant if it is taken away. We still speak of a property as a "holding", and "maintenance" means "holding in the hand". These words show the primitive connection between property and grasp; so does the word "grasping".

A child which has no toys of its own will pick up sticks or broken bricks or any odds and ends it may find, and will treasure them as its very own. The desire for property is so deep-seated that it cannot be thwarted without danger. Moreover property cultivates carefulness and curbs the impulse of destruction. Especially useful is property in anything that the child has made himself; if this is not permitted, his constructive impulses are checked.

Where the arguments are so conflicting, we cannot adopt any clear-cut policy, but must be guided to a great extent by circumstances and the child's nature. Nevertheless, something can be said as to the means of reconciling these opposites in practice.

Among toys, some should be private and some common. To take an extreme case, a rocking-horse would of course always be common. This suggests a principle: where a toy can be equally enjoyed by all, but only by one at a time, it should be common if it is too large or expensive to be duplicated. On the other hand, toys more adapted to one child than to another (because of difference of age, for example) may properly belong to the one to whom they give the most pleasure. If a toy wants careful handling which an older child has learnt to give, it is fair that a younger child should not be allowed to get hold of it and spoil it. The younger child should be compensated by private property in the toys specially appropriate to its age. After two years old, a broken toy should not be immediately replaced if it has been broken by the child's carelessness; it is just as well that the loss should be felt for a while. Do not let a child always refuse the use of its own toys to other children. Whenever it has more than it can actually use, it should not be allowed to protest if another child plays with those that it is not using. But here I should except toys which the other child is likely to break, and toys out of which their owner has constructed some edifice which is a source of pride. Until the edifice is forgotten, it should, if possible, be allowed to stand, as a reward of industry. Subject to these provisos, do not let the child develop a dog-in-the-manger attitude; it must never be allowed to prevent another child's enjoyment wantonly. It is not very difficult to teach a modicum of decent behaviour in these respects, and it is quite worth the necessary firmness. Do not allow a child to snatch things from another child, even when it would be within its legal rights in doing so. If an older child is unkind to a younger one, show a similar unkindness to the older one, and explain immediately why you do so. By such methods it is not difficult to establish that degree of kindness in children to each other which is necessary to prevent constant storms and tears. On occasion, a certain amount of sternness may be necessary, amounting to a mild form of punishment. But on no account must a habit of tyrannizing over the weak be allowed to develop.

While permitting a certain number of cherished possessions, it is well to encourage the habit of using toys, such as bricks, to which the child only has the exclusive right while he is using them. The Montessori apparatus is common to all the children, but so long as a child is using one piece of apparatus no other child must interfere. This develops a sense of limited tenant-right, dependent upon work; such a sense does not run counter to anything that is desirable in later years. For very young children, this method is hardly applicable, because they are not yet sufficiently constructive. But as they acquire skill it becomes more and more possible to interest them in the process of building. So long as they know they can have the material for construction whenever they like, they will not much mind others having it too, and the reluctance to sharing which they may feel at first is soon dispelled by custom. Nevertheless, when a child is old enough, he should, I think, be allowed to own books, because that will increase his love of books and therefore stimulate reading. The books that are his own property should, as far as possible be good books, such as Lewis Carroll and Tanglewood Tales, not mere trash. If the children want trash, it should be common property.

The broad principles involved are: First, do not produce in the child a sense of thwarting from not having enough property; this is the way to produce a miser. Secondly, allow the child private property when it stimulates a desirable activity, and, in particular, where it teaches careful handling. But subject to these limitations turn the child's attention, as far as you can, to pleasures not involving private ownership. And even where there is private ownership, do not allow the child to be mean or miserly when other children wish to be allowed to play with his things. As to this, however, the object is to induce the child to lend of his own free will; so long as authority is required the end aimed at has not been achieved. In a happy child, it should not be difficult to stimulate a generous disposition; but if the child is starved of pleasures, he will of course cling tenaciously to those that are attainable. It is not through suffering that children learn virtue, but through happiness and health.

TRUTHFULNESS

To produce the habit of truthfulness should be one of the major aims of moral education. I do not mean truthfulness in speech only, but also in thought; indeed, of the two, the latter seems to me the more important. I prefer a person who lies with full consciousness of what he is doing to a person who first sub-consciously deceives himself and then imagines that he is being virtuous and truthful. Indeed, no man who thinks truthfully can believe that it is *always* wrong to speak untruthfully. Those who hold that a lie is always wrong have to supplement this view by a great deal of casuistry and considerable practice in misleading ambiguities, by means of which they deceive without admitting to themselves that they are lying. Nevertheless, I hold that the occasions when lying is justifiable are few—much fewer than would be inferred from the practice of high-minded men. And almost all the occasions which justify lying are occasions where power is being used tyrannically, or where people are engaged in some harmful activity such as war, therefore in a good social system they would be even rarer than they are now.

Untruthfulness, as a practice, is almost always a product of fear. The child brought up without fear will be truthful, not in virtue of a moral effort, but because it will never occur to him to be otherwise. The child who has been treated wisely and kindly has a frank look in the eyes, and a fearless demeanour even with strangers; whereas the child that has been subject to nagging or severity is in perpetual terror of incurring reproof, and terrified of having transgressed some rule whenever he has behaved in a natural manner. It does not at first occur to a young child that it is possible to lie. The possibility of lying is a discovery, due to observation of grown-ups quickened by terror. The child discovers that grown-ups lie to him, and that it is dangerous to tell them the truth; under these circumstances he takes to lying. Avoid these incentives, and he will not think of lying.

But in judging whether children are truthful, a certain caution is necessary. Children's memories are very faulty, and they often do not know the answer to a question when grown-up people think they do. Their sense of time is very vague; a child under four will hardly distinguish between yesterday and a week ago, or between yesterday and six hours ago. When they do not know the answer to a question, they tend to say yes or no according to the suggestion in your tone of voice. Again, they are often talking in the dramatic character of some make-believe. When they tell you solemnly that there is a lion in the back garden, this is obvious; but in many cases it is quite easy to mistake play for earnest. For all these reasons, a young child's statements are often objectively untrue, but without the slightest intention to deceive. Indeed, children tend, at first, to regard grown-ups as omniscient, and therefore incapable of being deceived. My boy (three and three quarters) will ask me to tell him (for the pleasure of the story) what occurred to him on some interesting occasion when I was not present; I find it almost impossible to persuade him that I don't know what happened. Grown-up people get to know so many things in ways the child does not understand, that he cannot set limits to their powers. Last Easter, my boy was given a number of chocolate Easter eggs. We told him that if he ate too much chocolate he would be sick, but, having told him, we left him alone. He ate too much, and was sick. He came to me as soon as the crisis was over, with a beaming face, saying, in a voice almost of triumph, "I was sick, Daddy—Daddy told me I should be sick." His pleasure in the verification of a scientific law was astonishing. Since then, it has been possible to trust him with chocolate, in spite of the fact that he seldom has it; moreover he implicitly believes everything we tell him about what food is good for him. There has been no need of moral exhortation or punishment or fear in bringing about this result. There has been need, at earlier stages, of patience and firmness. He is nearing the age where it is usual for boys to steal sweet things and lie about it. I dare say he will steal sometimes, but I shall be surprised if he lies. When a child does lie, parents should take themselves to task rather than him; they should deal with it by removing its causes, and by explaining gently and reasonably why it is better not to lie. They should not deal with it by punishment, which only increases fear and therefore the motive for lying.

Rigid truthfulness in adults towards children is, of course, absolutely indispensable if children are not to learn lying. Parents who teach that lying is a sin, and who nevertheless are known to lie by their children, naturally lose all moral authority. The idea of speaking the truth to children is entirely novel; hardly anybody did it before the present generation. I greatly doubt whether Eve told Cain and Abel the truth about apples; I am convinced that she told them she had never eaten anything that wasn't good

Another undesirable form of humbug is to treat inanimate objects as if they were alive. Nurses sometimes teach children, when they have hurt themselves by bumping into a chair or table, to smack the offending object and say, "naughty chair" or "naughty table". This removes a most useful source of natural discipline. Left to himself, the child soon realizes that inanimate objects can only be manipulated by skill, not by anger or cajolery. This is a stimulus to the acquisition of skill, and a help in realizing the limits of personal power.

Lies about sex are sanctioned by time-honoured usage. I believe them to be wholly and utterly bad, but I shall say no more on this subject now, as I propose to devote a chapter to sex education.

Children who are not suppressed ask innumerable questions, some intelligent, others quite the reverse. These questions are often wearisome, and sometimes inconvenient. But they must be answered truthfully, to the best of your ability. If the child asks you a question connected with religion, say exactly what you think, even if you contradict some other grown-up person who thinks differently. If he asks you about death, answer him. If he asks you questions designed to show that you are wicked or foolish, answer him. If he asks you about war, or capital punishment, answer him. Do not put him off with "you can't understand that yet", except in difficult scientific matters, such as how electric light is made. And even then, make it clear that the answer is a pleasure in store for him, as soon as he has learnt rather more than he now knows. Tell him rather more than he can understand, not rather less; the part he fails to understand will stimulate his curiosity and his intellectual ambition.

Invariable truthfulness to a child reaps its reward in increased trust. The child has a natural tendency to believe what you say, except when it runs counter to a strong desire, as in the case of the Easter eggs which I mentioned just now. A little experience of the truth of your remarks even in these cases enables you to win belief easily and without emphasis. But if you have been in the habit of threatening consequences which did not happen, you will have to become more and more insistent and terrifying, and in the end you will only produce a state of nervous uncertainty. One day my boy wanted to paddle in a stream, but I told him not to, because I thought there were bits of broken crockery which would cut his feet. His desire was keen, so he was sceptical about the crockery; but after I had found a piece and shown him the sharp edge, he became entirely acquiescent. If I had invented the crockery for my own convenience, I should have lost his confidence. If I had not found any, I should have let him paddle. In consequence of repeated experiences of this sort, he has almost entirely ceased to be sceptical of my reasons.

We live in a world of humbug, and the child brought up without humbug is bound to despise much that is commonly thought to deserve respect. This is regrettable, because contempt is a bad emotion. I should not call his attention to such matters, though I should satisfy his curiosity whenever it turned towards them. Truthfulness is something of a handicap in a hypocritical society, but the handicap is more than outweighed by the advantages of fearlessness, without which no one can be truthful. We wish our children to be upright, candid, frank, self-respecting; for my part, I would rather see them fail with these qualities than succeed by the arts of the slave. A certain native pride and integrity is essential to a splendid human being, and where it exists lying becomes impossible, except when it is prompted by some generous motive. I would have my children truthful in their thoughts and words, even if it should entail worldly misfortune, for something of more importance than riches and honours is at stake.

PUNISHMENT

IN former days, and until very recently, the punishment of children, both boys and girls, was taken as a matter of course, and was universally regarded as indispensable in education. We have seen in an earlier chapter what Dr. Arnold thought about flogging, and his views were, at the time, exceptionally humane. Rousseau is associated with the theory of leaving things to nature, yet in "Emile" he occasionally advocates quite severe punishments. The conventional view, a hundred years ago, is set forth in one of the "Cautionary Tales", in which a little girl makes a fuss because they are putting on her white sash when she wants her pink one.

> Papa, who in the parlour heard
> Her make the noise and rout,
> That instant went to Caroline,
> To whip her, there's no doubt.

When Mr. Fairchild found his children quarrelling, he caned them, making the cane keep time to the verse "Let dogs delight to bark and bite". He then took them to see a corpse hanging in chains on a gibbet. The little boy was frightened, and begged to be taken home, as the chains rattled in the wind. But Mr. Fairchild compelled him to look for a long time, saying that this spectacle showed what happened to those who had hatred in their hearts. The child was destined to become a clergyman, and presumably had to be taught to depict the terrors of the damned with the vividness of one who has experienced them.

Nowadays, few people would advocate such methods, even in Tennessee. But there is considerable divergence of opinion as to what should take their place. Some people still advocate a fair amount of punishment, while others consider that it is possible to dispense with punishment altogether. There is room for many shades between these two extremes.

For my part, I believe that punishment has a certain very minor place in education; but I doubt whether it need ever be severe. I include speaking sharply or reprovingly among punishments. The most severe punishment that ought ever to be necessary is the natural spontaneous expression of indignation. On a few occasions when my boy has been rough with his younger sister, his mother has expressed anger by an impulsive exclamation. The effect has been very great. The boy burst into sobs, and would not be consoled until his mother had made much of him. The impression was very profound, as one could see from his subsequent good conduct towards his sister. On a few occasions we have resorted to mild forms of punishment when he has persisted in demanding things we had refused him, or in interfering with his sister's play. In such cases, when reason and exhortation have failed, we take him to a room by himself, leave the door open, and tell him he can come back as soon as he is good. In a very few minutes, after crying vigorously, he comes back, and is invariably good: he perfectly understands that in coming back he has undertaken to be good. So far, we have never found any need of severer penalties. If one can judge from the books of old-fashioned disciplinarians, the children educated by the old methods were far naughtier than the modern child. I should certainly be horrified if my boy were half as badly behaved as the children in "The Fairchild Family"; but I should think the fault lay more with his parents than with himself. I believe that reasonable parents create reasonable children. The children must feel their parents' affection—not duty and responsibility, for which no child is grateful, but warm love, which feels delight in the child's presence and ways. And except when it is quite impossible, a prohibition must be explained carefully and truthfully. Small misfortunes, such as bruises and slight cuts, should sometimes be allowed to happen rather than interfere with rash games; a little experience of this kind makes children more willing to believe that a prohibition may be wise. Where these conditions are present from the first, I believe children will seldom do anything deserving of serious punishment.

When a child persistently interferes with other children or spoils their pleasures, the obvious penalty is banishment. It is imperatively necessary to take steps of some kind, because it would be most unfair to let the other children suffer. But there is no use in making the refractory child feel guilty; it is much more to the purpose to make him feel that he is missing pleasures which the others are enjoying. Madame Montessori describes her practice as follows:

As to punishments, we have many times come in contact with children who disturbed the others without paying attention to our corrections. Such children were at once examined by the physician. When the case proved to be that of a normal child, we placed one of the little tables in a corner of the room, and in this way isolated the child; having him sit in a comfortable little armchair, so placed that he might see his companions at work, and giving him those games and toys to which he was most attracted. This isolation almost always succeeded in calming the child; from his position he could see the entire assembly of his companions, and the way in which they carried on their work was an *object lesson* much more efficacious than any words of the teacher could possibly have been. Little by little, he would come to see the advantages of being one of the company working so busily before his eyes, and he would really wish to go back and do as the others did. We have in this way led back again to discipline all the children who at first seemed to rebel against it. The isolated child was always made the object of special care, almost as if he were ill. I myself, when I entered the room, went first of all directly to him, as if he were a very little child. Then I turned my attention to the others, interesting myself in their work, asking questions about it as if they had been little men. I do not know what happened in the soul of these children whom we found it necessary to discipline, but certainly the conversion was always very complete and lasting. They showed great pride in learning how to work and how to conduct themselves, and always showed a very tender affection for the teacher and for me.[1]

The success of this method depended upon several factors not present in old-fashioned schools. There was first the elimination of those whose bad conduct was due to some medical defect. Then there was tact and skill in applying the method. But the really vital point was the good conduct of the majority of the class: the child felt itself opposed to the public opinion which it naturally respected.

[1] "The Montessori Method" (Heinemann, 1912), p. 103.

This is, of course, an entirely different situation from that of the schoolmaster who has a class bent on "ragging". I do not propose to discuss the methods which he should employ, because they would never be needed if education were properly conducted from the start. Children like to learn things, provided they are the right things properly taught. The same mistake is made in imparting knowledge as is made, at an earlier stage, in regard to food and sleep: something which is really an advantage to the child is made to appear like a favour to the adult. Infants easily come to think that the only reason for eating and sleeping is that grown-ups desire it; this turns them into dyspeptic sufferers from insomnia.[2] Unless a child is ill, let it leave its food and go hungry. My boy had been coaxed into eating by his nurse, and had grown more and more *difficile*. One day when we had him for his mid-day meal, he refused to eat his pudding, so we sent it out. After a while, he demanded it back, but it turned out that the cook had eaten it. He was flabbergasted, and never made such pretences with us again. Exactly the same method should apply to instruction. Those who do not want it should be allowed to go without, though I should see to it that they were bored if they were absent during lesson time. If they see

[2] See Dr. H. C. Cameron, "The Nervous Child", Chaps. IV and V.

others learning, they will presently clamour to be taught: the teacher can then appear as conferring a benefit, which is the truth of the situation. I should have in every school a large bare room to which pupils could go if they did not want to learn, but if they went there, I should not allow them to come back to lessons that day. And they should be sent there as a punishment if they behaved badly in lesson-time. It seems a simple principle that a punishment should be something you wish the culprit to dislike, not something you wish him to like. Yet "lines" are a common punishment where the professed aim is to produce a love of classical literature.

Mild punishments have their utility for dealing with mild offences, especially such as are concerned with manners. Praise and blame are an important form of rewards and punishments for young children, and also for older boys and girls if conferred by a person who inspires respect. I do not believe it possible to conduct education without praise and blame, but in regard to both a certain degree of caution is necessary. In the first place, neither should be comparative. A child should not be told that he has done better than so-and-so, or that such-and-such is never naughty: the first produces contempt, the second hatred. In the second place, blame should be given much more sparingly than praise; it should be a definite punishment, administered for some unexpected lapse from good behaviour, and it should never be continued after it has produced its effect. In the third place, praise should not be given for anything that should be a matter of course. I should give it for a new development of courage or skill, and for an act of unselfishness as regards possessions, if achieved after a moral effort. All through education, any unusually good piece of work should be praised. To be praised for a difficult achievement is one of the most delightful experiences in youth, and the desire for this pleasure is quite proper as an added incentive, though it should not be the main motive. The main motive should always be an interest in the matter itself, whatever the matter may happen to be.

Grave faults of character, such as cruelty, can seldom be dealt with by means of punishment. Or rather, punishment should be a very small part of the treatment. Cruelty to animals is more or less natural to boys, and requires, for its prevention, an education *ad hoc*. It is a very bad plan to wait until you find your boy torturing an animal, and then proceed to torture the boy. This only makes him wish he had not been caught. You should watch for the first beginnings of what may afterwards develop into cruelty. Teach the boy respect for life; do not let him see you killing animals, even wasps or snakes. If you cannot prevent it, explain very carefully why it is done in this particular case. If he does something slightly unkind to a younger child, do the same to him at once. He will protest, and you can explain that if he does not want it done to him he must not do it to others. In this way the fact that others have feelings like his own is brought vividly to his attention.

It is obviously essential to this method that it should be begun early, and applied to minor forms of unkindness. It is only very small injuries to others that you can retort in kind upon the child. And when you can adopt this plan, do not let it seem that you are doing it as a punishment, but rather as an instruction: "See, that is what you did to your little sister." When the child protests, you say: "Well, if it was unpleasant, you mustn't do it to her." So long as the whole incident is simple and immediate, the child will understand, and will learn that other people's feelings must be considered. In that case, serious cruelty will never develop.

All moral instruction must be immediate and concrete: it must arise out of a situation which has grown up naturally, and must not go beyond what ought to be done in this particular instance. The child himself will apply the moral in other similar cases. It is much easier to grasp a concrete instance, and apply analogous considerations to an analogous instance, than to apprehend a general rule and proceed deductively. Do not say, in a general way, "Be brave, be kind", but urge him to some particular piece of daring, and then say, "Bravo, you were a brave boy"; get him to let his sister play with his mechanical engine, and when he sees her beaming with delight, say, "That's right, you were a kind boy." The same principle applies in dealing with cruelty: Look out for its faint beginnings, and prevent them from developing.

If, in spite of all your efforts, grave cruelty develops at a later age, the matter must be taken very seriously, and dealt with like an illness. The boy should be punished in the sense that unpleasant things should happen to him, just as they do when he has measles, but not in the sense that he should be made to feel wicked. He should be isolated for a while from other children and from animals, and it should be explained to him that it is not safe to let him associate with them. He should be made to realize, as far as possible, how he would suffer if he were cruelly treated. He should be made to feel that a great misfortune had befallen him in the shape of an impulse to cruelty, and that his elders were endeavouring to shield him from a similar misfortune in the future. I believe that such methods would be completely successful in all except a few pathological cases.

Physical punishment I believe to be never right. In mild forms, it does little harm, though no good; in severe forms, I am convinced that it generates cruelty and brutality. It is true that it oftens produces no resentment against the person who inflicts it; where it is customary, boys adapt themselves to it and expect it as part of the course of nature. But it accustoms them to the idea that it may be right and proper to inflict physical pain for the purpose of maintaining authority—a peculiarly dangerous lesson to teach to those who are likely to acquire positions of power. And it destroys that relation of open confidence which ought to exist between parents and children, as well as between teachers and pupils. The modern parent wants his children to be as unconstrained in his presence as in his absence; he wants them to feel pleasure when they see him coming; he does not want a fictitious Sabbath calm while he is watching, succeeded by pandemonium as soon as he turns his back. To win the genuine affection of children is a joy as great as any that life has to offer. Our grandfathers did not know of this joy, and therefore did not know that they were missing it. They taught children that it was their "duty" to love their parents, and proceeded to make this duty almost impossible of performance. Caroline, in the verse quoted at the beginning of this chapter, can hardly have been pleased when her father went to her, "to whip her, there's no doubt". So long as people persisted in the notion that love could be commanded as a duty, they did nothing to win it as a genuine emotion. Consequently human relations remained stark and harsh and cruel. Punishment was part of this whole conception. It is strange that men who would not have dreamed of raising their hand against a woman were quite willing to inflict physical torture upon a defenceless child. Mercifully, a better conception of the relations of parents and children has gradually won its way during the last hundred years, and with it the whole theory of punishment has been transformed. I hope that the enlightened ideas which begin to prevail in education will gradually spread to other human relations as well, for they are needed there just as much as in our dealings with our children.

So far, we have been considering what parents and teachers can do themselves towards creating the right kind of character in a child. But there is a great deal that cannot possibly be done without the help of other children. This becomes increasingly true as the child gets older; indeed contemporaries are never more important than at the university. In the first year of life, other children are not important at all in the earlier months, and only a slight advantage in the last three months. At that stage, it is slightly older children that are useful. The first child in a family is usually slower in learning to walk and talk than subsequent children, because grown-ups are so perfect in these accomplishments that they are difficult to imitate. A child of three years old is a better model for a child one year old, both because the things it does are more what the younger child would wish to do, and because its powers do not seem so superhuman. Children feel that other children are more akin to them than adults are,

102

and therefore their ambition is more stimulated by what other children do. Only the family provides the opportunity for this early education by older children. Most children who have a choice wish to play with children rather older than themselves, because then they feel "grand"; but these older children wish to play with still older children, and so on. The consequence is that, in a school, or in the streets of a slum, or anywhere else where a large choice is possible, children play almost entirely with their contemporaries, because the older ones will not play with the younger ones. In this way it comes about that what is to be learnt from older children must be learnt mainly in the home. This has the drawback that in every family there must be one oldest child, who fails to get the benefits of the method. And as families grow smaller, the percentage of oldest children grows larger, so that the drawback is an increasing one. Small families are in some ways a disadvantage to children, unless supplemented by nursery schools. But nursery schools will form the subject of a later chapter.

Older children, younger children, and contemporaries all have their uses, but the uses of older and younger children, for the reasons just given, are mainly confined to the family. The great use of older children is to provide attainable ambitions. A child will make tremendous efforts to be thought worthy of joining in an older child's game. The older child behaves in an offhand natural way, without the consideration and make-believe which is bound to form part of a grown-up person's games with children. The same lack of consideration in a grown-up would be painful, both because the grown-up has power and authority, and because he plays to please the child, not to please himself. A child will be cheerfully submissive to an older brother or sister, in a way which would be impossible towards an adult except as a result of excessive discipline. The lesson of co-operation in a subordinate role is best learnt from other children; when grown-ups try to teach it, they are faced with the opposite dangers of unkindness and pretence—unkindness if they demand real co-operation, pretence if they are content with the appearance of it. I do not mean that either real or pretence co-operation is to be always avoided, but that it has not the spontaneity which is possible between an older and a younger child, and therefore cannot be combined for hours on end with pleasure to both parties.

All through youth, slightly older people continue to have a special use in teaching—not formal teaching, but the sort which occurs outside working hours. A slightly older boy or girl remains always a very effective stimulus to ambition, and, if kind, can explain difficulties better than an adult, from the recent recollection of overcoming them. Even at the university, I learnt much from people a few years senior to me, which I could not have learnt from grave and reverend signors. I believe this experience is general wherever the social life of the university is not too rigidly stratified by "years". It is, of course, impossible where, as too often happens, the older students consider it *infra dig* to have anything to do with the younger ones.

Younger children also have their uses, especially in the years from three to six; these uses are chiefly in connection with moral education. So long as a child is with adults, it has no occasion for the exercise of a number of important virtues, namely, those required by the strong in dealing with the weak. A child has to be taught not to take things by force from a younger brother or sister, not to show excessive anger when the junior inadvertently knocks over his tower of bricks, not to hoard toys he is not using which the other desires. He has to be taught that the junior can be easily hurt by rough handling, and to feel compunction when he has wantonly caused tears. In protecting a younger child, one can speak to the senior with a sharpness and suddenness which would not otherwise be justified, but which have their uses through the strong impression produced by their unexpectedness. All these are useful lessons, which it is hardly possible to give naturally in any other way. It is a folly and a waste of time to give abstract moral instruction to a child; everything must be concrete, and actually demanded by the existing situation. Much that, from an adult point of view, is moral education, feels to the child just like instruction in handling a saw. The child feels that he is being shown how the thing is done. That is one reason why example is so important. A child who has watched a carpenter at work tries to copy his movements; a child who has seen his parents behaving always with kindness and consideration tries to copy them in this respect. In each case, prestige is attached to what he wants to imitate. If you gave your child a solemn lesson in the use of a saw, but yourself always tried to use it as a chopper, you would never make a carpenter of him. And if you urge him to be kind to his little sister, but are not kind to her yourself, all your instruction will be wasted. For that reason, when you have to do something that makes a little child cry, such as cleaning its nose, you should be careful to explain to the older child why it is necessary to do it. Otherwise he is quite likely to rise up in defence of the younger child, and fight you to make you stop being cruel. If you allow him to remain under the impression that you are cruel, you will have lost the power to curb his own impulses towards tyranny.

Although both older and younger children are important, contemporaries are far more so, at any rate from the age of four onwards. Behaviour to equals is what most needs to be learnt. Most of the inequalities in the existing world are artificial, and it would be a good thing if our behaviour ignored them. Well-to-do people imagine themselves superior to their cooks, and behave to them in a different way from that in which they behave in society. But they feel inferior to a Duke, and treat him in a way which shows a lack of self-respect. In both cases they are wrong: the cook and the Duke should both be felt and treated as equals. In youth, age makes a hierarchy which is not artificial; but for that very reason the social habits which will be desirable in later life are best learnt by associating with contemporaries. Games of all kinds are better among equals, and so is school competition. Among schoolfellows, a boy has that degree of importance which is accorded to him by their judgment; he may be admired or despised, but the issue depends upon his own character and prowess. Affectionate parents create a too indulgent milieu; parents without affection create one where spontaneity is repressed. It is only contemporaries who can give scope for spontaneity in free competition and in equal co-operation. Self-respect without tyranny, consideration without slavishness, can be learnt best in dealing with equals. For these reasons, no amount of parental solicitude can give a boy or girl the same advantages at home as are to be enjoyed in a good school.

Apart from these considerations, there is another, perhaps even more important. The mind and body of a child demand a great deal of play, and after the first years play can hardly be satisfactory except with other boys and girls. Without play, a child becomes strained and nervous; it loses the joy of life and develops anxieties. It is, of course, possible to bring up a child as John Stuart Mill was brought up, to begin Greek at the age of three, and never know any ordinary childish fun. From the mere standpoint of acquiring knowledge, the results may be good, but taken all round I cannot admire them. Mill relates in his Autobiography that during adolescence he nearly committed suicide from the thought that all combinations of musical notes would one day be used up, and then new musical composition would become impossible. It is obvious that an obsession of this sort is a symptom of nervous exhaustion. In later life, whenever he came upon an argument tending to show that his father's philosophy might have been mistaken, he shied away from it like a frightened horse, thereby greatly diminishing the value of his reasoning powers. It seems probable that a more normal youth would have given him more intellectual resilience, and enabled him to be more original in his thinking. However that may be, it would certainly have given him more capacity for enjoying life. I was myself the product of a solitary education up to the age of sixteen—somewhat less fierce than Mill's, but still too destitute of the ordinary joys of youth. I experienced in adolescence just the same tendency to suicide as Mill describes—in my case, because I thought the laws of dynamics regulated the movements of my body, making the will a mere delusion. When I began to associate with contemporaries, I found myself an angular prig. How far I have remained so, it is not for me to say.

In spite of all the above arguments, I am prepared to admit that there are a certain number of boys and girls who ought not to go to school, and that some of them are very important individuals. If a boy has abnormal mental powers in some direction, combined with poor physique and great nervousness, he may be quite incapable of fitting into a crowd of normal boys, and may be so persecuted as to be driven mad. Exceptional capacities are not infrequently associated with mental instability, and in such cases it is desirable to adopt methods which would be bad for the normal boy. Care should be taken to find out if abnormal sensitiveness has some definite cause, and patient efforts should be made to cure it. But these efforts should never involve terrible suffering, such as an abnormal boy may easily have to endure from brutal companions. I think such sensitiveness generally has its source in mistakes during infancy, which have upset the child's digestion or its nerves. Given wisdom in handling infants, I think almost all of them would grow into boys and girls sufficiently normal to enjoy the company of other boys and girls. Nevertheless, some exceptions will occur, and they may easily occur among those who have some form of genius. In these rare cases, school is undesirable, and a more sheltered youth is to be preferred.

AFFECTION AND SYMPATHY

MANY readers may think that I have hitherto unaccountably neglected affection, which is, in some sense, the essence of a good character. I hold that love and knowledge are the two main requisites for right action, yet, in dealing with moral education, I have hitherto said nothing about love. My reason has been that the right sort of love should be the natural fruit resulting from the proper treatment of the growing child, rather than something consciously aimed at throughout the various stages. We have to be clear as to the kind of affection to be desired, and as to the disposition appropriate to different ages. From ten or twelve years old until puberty, a boy is apt to be very destitute of affection, and there is nothing to be gained by trying to force his nature. Throughout youth, there is less occasion for sympathy than in adult life, both because there is less power of giving effective expression to it, and because a young person has to think of his or her own training for life, largely to the exclusion of other people's interests. For these reasons, we should be more concerned to produce sympathetic and affectionate adults than to force a precocious development of these qualities in early years. Our problem, like all problems in the education of character, is a scientific one, belonging to what may be called psychological dynamics. Love cannot exist as a duty: to tell a child that it *ought* to love its parents and its brothers and sisters is utterly useless, if not worse. Parents who wish to be loved must behave so as to elicit love, and must try to give to their children those physical and mental characteristics which produce expansive affections.

Not only must children not be commanded to love their parents, but nothing must be done which has this result as its object. Parental affection, at its best, differs from sex love in this respect. It is of the essence of sex love to seek a response, as is natural, since, without a response, it cannot fulfil its biological function. But it is not of the essence of parental love to seek a response. The natural unsophisticated parental instinct feels towards the child as towards an externalized part of the parent's body. If your great toe is out of order, you attend to it from self-interest, and you do not expect it to feel grateful. The savage woman, I imagine, has a very similar feeling towards her child. She desires its welfare in just the same way as she desires her own, especially while it is still very young. She has no more sense of self-denial in looking after the child than in looking after herself; and for that very reason she does not look for gratitude. The child's need of her is sufficient response so long as it is helpless. Later, when it begins to grow up, her affection diminishes and her demands may increase. In animals, parental affection ceases when the child is adult, and no demands are made upon it; but in human beings, even if they are very primitive, this is not the case. A son who is a lusty warrior is expected to feed and protect his parents when they are old and decrepit; the story of Æneas and Anchises embodies this feeling at a higher level of culture. With the growth of foresight, there is an increasing tendency to exploit children's affections for the sake of their help when old age comes. Hence the principle of filial piety, which has existed throughout the world and is embodied in the Fifth Commandment. With the development of private property and ordered government, filial piety becomes less important; after some centuries, people become aware of this fact, and the sentiment goes out of fashion. In the modern world, a man of fifty may be financially dependent upon a parent of eighty, so that the important thing is still the affection of the parent for the child rather than of the child for the parent. This, of course, applies chiefly to the propertied classes; among wage-earners, the older relationship persists. But even there it is being gradually displaced as a result of old-age pensions and similar measures. Affection of children for parents, therefore, is ceasing to deserve a place among cardinal virtues, while affection of parents for children remains of enormous importance.

There is another set of dangers, which has been brought to the fore by the psycho-analysts, though I think their interpretation of the facts may be questioned. The dangers I am thinking of are those connected with undue devotion to one or other parent. An adult, and even an adolescent, ought not to be so overshadowed by either father or mother as to be unable to think or feel independently. This may easily happen if the personality of the parent is stronger than that of the child. I do not believe that there is, except in rare morbid cases, an "Œdipus Complex", in the sense of a special attraction of sons to mothers and daughters to fathers. The excessive influence of the parent, where it exists, will belong to the parent who has had most to do with the child—generally the mother—without regard to difference of sex. Of course, it may happen that a daughter who dislikes her mother and sees little of her father will idealize the latter; but in that case the influence is exerted by dreams, not by the actual father. Idealization consists of hanging hopes to a peg: the peg is merely convenient, and has nothing to do with the nature of the hopes. Undue parental influence is quite a different thing from this, since it is connected with the actual person, not with an imaginary portrait.

An adult with whom a child is in constant contact may easily become so dominant in the child's life as to make the child, even in later life, a mental slave. The slavery may be intellectual, or emotional, or both. A good example of the former is John Stuart Mill, who could never bring himself, in the last resort, to admit that his father might have been mistaken. To some degree, intellectual slavery to early environment is normal; very few adults are capable of opinions other than those taught by parents or teachers, except where there is some general drift that carries them along. The children of Mohammedans are Mohammedans, the children of Buddhists are Buddhists, and so on. It may be maintained that intellectual slavery is natural and normal; I am inclined to admit that it can only be avoided by an education *ad hoc*. This form of excessive parental and scholastic influence ought to be avoided carefully, since, in a rapidly changing world, it is exceedingly dangerous to retain the opinions of a by-gone generation. But for the present

I shall consider only slavery of the emotions and the will, since that is more directly bound up with our present topic.

The evils considered by psycho-analysts under the heading "Œdipus Complex" (which I regard as misleading) arise from an undue desire on the part of parents for an emotional response from their children. As I said a moment ago, I believe that the parental instinct in its purity does not desire an emotional response; it is satisfied by the dependence of the young, and the fact that they look to parents for protection and food. When the dependence ceases, parental affection also ceases. This is the state of affairs among animals, and for their purposes it is entirely satisfactory. But such simplicity of instinct is scarcely possible for human beings. I have already considered the effect of military and economic considerations, as shown in the preaching of filial piety. I am now concerned with two purely psychological sources of confusion in the working of the parental instinct.

The first of these is of a sort which occurs wherever intelligence observes the pleasures to be derived from instinct. Broadly speaking, instinct prompts pleasant acts which have useful consequences, but the consequences may not be pleasant. Eating is pleasant, but digestion is not—especially when it is indigestion. Sex is pleasant, but parturition is not. The dependence of an infant is pleasant, but the independence of a vigorous grown-up son is not. The primitive maternal type of woman derives most pleasure from the infant at the breast, and gradually less pleasure as the child grows less helpless. There is therefore a tendency, for the sake of pleasure, to prolong the period of helplessness, and to put off the time when the child can dispense with parental guidance. This is recognized in conventional phrases, such as being "tied to his mother's apron-strings". It was thought impossible to deal with this evil in boys except by sending them away to school. In girls it was not recognized as an evil, because (if they were well-to-do) it was thought desirable to make them helpless and dependent, and it was hoped that after marriage they would cling to their husbands as they had formerly clung to their mothers. This seldom happened, and its failure gave rise to the "mother-in-law" joke. One of the purposes of a joke is to prevent thought—a purpose in which this particular joke was highly successful. No one seemed to realize that a girl brought up to be dependent would naturally be dependent upon her mother, and therefore could not enter into that wholehearted partnership with a man which is the essence of a happy marriage.

The second psychological complication comes

nearer to the orthodox Freudian point of view. It arises where elements appropriate to sex-love enter into parental affection. I do not mean anything necessarily dependent upon difference of sex; I mean merely the desire for a certain kind of emotional response. Part of the psychology of sex—that part, in fact, which has made monogamy a possible institution—is the desire to come first for some one, to feel that oneself is more important than any other human being to the happiness of at least one person in the world. When this desire has produced marriage, it will only produce happiness if a number of other conditions are realized. For one reason or another, a very large proportion of married women in civilized countries fail to have a satisfying sex-life. When this happens to a woman, she is apt to seek from her children an illegitimate and spurious gratification of desires which only men can gratify adequately and naturally. I do not mean anything obvious: I mean merely a certain emotional tension, a certain passionateness of feeling, a pleasure in kissing and fondling to excess. These things used to be thought quite right and proper in an affectionate mother. Indeed, the difference between what is right and what is harmful is very subtle. It is absurd to maintain, as some Freudians do, that parents ought not to kiss and fondle their children at all. Children have a right to warm affection from their parents; it gives them a happy, care-free outlook upon the world, and is essential to healthy psychological development. But it should be something that they take for granted, like the air they breathe, not something to which they are expected to respond. It is this question of response that is the essence of the matter. There will be a certain spontaneous response, which is all to the good; but it will be quite different from the active pursuit of friendship from childish companions. Psychologically, parents should be a background, and the child should not be made to act with a view to giving his parents pleasure. Their pleasure should consist in his growth and progress; anything that he gives them in the way of response should be accepted gratefully as a pure extra, like fine weather in spring, but should not be expected as part of the order of nature.

It is very difficult for a woman to be a perfect mother, or a perfect teacher of young children, unless she is sexually satisfied. Whatever psycho-analysts may say, the parental instinct is essentially different from the sex instinct, and is damaged by the intrusion of emotions appropriate to sex. The habit of employing celibate female teachers is quite wrong psychologically. The right woman to deal with children is a woman whose instinct is not seeking from them satisfactions for herself which they ought not to be expected to provide. A woman who is happily married will belong to this type without effort; but any other woman will need an almost impossible subtlety of self-control. Of course, the same thing applies to men in the same circumstances, but the circumstances are far less frequent with men, both because their parental instincts are usually not very strong, and because they are seldom sexually starved.

It is as well to be clear in our own thoughts as regards the attitude we are to expect from children to parents. If parents have the right kind of love for their children, the children's response will be just what the parents desire. The children will be pleased when their parents come, and sorry when they go, unless they are absorbed in some agreeable pursuit; they will look to their parents for help in any trouble, physical or mental, that may arise; they will dare to be adventurous, because they rely upon their parents' protection in the background— but this feeling will be hardly conscious except in moments of peril. They will expect their parents to answer their questions, resolve their perplexities, and help them in difficult tasks. Most of what their parents do for them will not enter into their consciousness. They will like their parents, not for providing their board and lodging, but for playing with them, showing

hem how to do new things, and telling them
tories about the world. They will gradually
realize that their parents love them, but this
ought to be accepted as a natural fact. The
affection that they feel for their parents will be
quite a different kind from that which they feel
for other children. The parent must act with
reference to the child, but the child must act
with reference to himself and the outer world.
That is the essential difference. The child has
no important function to perform in relation
to his parents. His function is to grow in wisdom and stature, and so long as he does so a
healthy parental instinct is satisfied.

I should be very sorry to convey the impression that I want to diminish the amount of affection in family life, or the spontaneity of its
manifestations. That is not at all what I mean.
What I do mean is that there are different kinds
of affection. The affection of husband and
wife is one thing, that of parents for children is
another, and that of children for parents is yet
another. The harm comes when these different
kinds of natural affection are confused. I do
not think the Freudians have arrived at the
truth, because they do not recognize these instinctive differences. And this makes them, in
a sense, ascetic as regards parents and children,
because they view any love between them as a
sort of inadequate sex-love. I do not believe

in the need of any fundamental self-denial, provided there are no special unfortunate circumstances. A man and woman who love each other and their children ought to be able to act spontaneously as the heart dictates. They will need much thought and knowledge, but these they will acquire out of parental affection. They must not demand from their children what they get from each other, but if they are happy in each other they will feel no impulse to do so. If the children are properly cared for they will feel for their parents a natural affection which will be no barrier to independence. What is needed is not ascetic self-denial but freedom and expansiveness of instinct adequately informed by intelligence and knowledge.

When my boy was two years and four months old, I went to America, and was absent three months. He was perfectly happy in my absence, but was wild with joy when I returned. I found him waiting impatiently by the garden gate; he seized my hand, and began showing me everything that specially interested him. I wanted to hear, and he wanted to tell; I had no wish to tell, and he had none to hear. The two impulses were different, but harmonious. When it comes to stories, he wishes to hear and I wish to tell, so that again there is harmony. Only once has this situation been reversed. When he was three years and six months old, I had a birthday, and his mother told him that everything was to be done to please me. Stories are his supreme delight; to our surprise, when the time for them came, he announced that he was going to tell me stories, as it was my birthday. He told about a dozen, then jumped down, saying "no more stories to-day". That was three months ago, but he has never told stories again.

I come now to the wider question of affection and sympathy in general. As between parents and children, there are complications owing to the possibility of abuse of power by parents; it was necessary to deal with these complications before attacking the general question.

There is no possible method of *compelling* a child to feel sympathy or affection; the only possible method is to observe the conditions under which these feelings arise spontaneously, and then endeavour to produce the conditions. Sympathy, undoubtedly, is partly instinctive. Children are worried when their brothers or sisters cry, and often cry too. They will take their part vehemently against the grown-ups when disagreeable things are being done to them. When my boy had a wound on his elbow which had to be dressed, his sister (aged eighteen months) could hear him crying in another room, and was very much upset. She kept on repeating "Jonny crying, Jonny crying", until the painful business was finished. When my boy saw his mother extracting a thorn with a needle from her foot, he said anxiously, "It doesn't hurt, Mummy". She said it did, wishing to give him a lesson in not making a fuss. He insisted that it didn't hurt, whereupon she insisted that it did. He then burst into sobs just as vehement as if it had been his own foot. Such occurrences must spring from instinctive physical sympathy. This is the basis upon which more elaborate forms of sympathy must be built. It is clear that nothing further is needed in the way of positive education except to bring home to the child the fact that people and animals can feel pain, and do feel it under certain circumstances. There is, however, a further negative condition: the child must not see people he respects committing unkind or cruel actions. If the father shoots or the mother speaks rudely to the maids, the child will catch these vices.

It is a difficult question how and when to make a child aware of the evil in the world. It is impossible to grow up ignorant of wars and massacres and poverty and preventable disease which is not prevented. At some stage, the child must know of these things, and must combine the knowledge with a firm conviction that t is a dreadful thing to inflict, or even permit, any suffering which can be avoided. We are here confronted by a problem similar to that which faces people who wish to preserve female chastity; these people formerly believed in ignorance till marriage, but now adopt more positive methods.

I have known some pacifists who wished history taught without reference to wars, and thought that children should be kept as long as possible ignorant of the cruelty in the world. But I cannot praise the "fugitive and cloistered virtue" that depends upon absence of knowledge. As soon as history is taught at all, it should be taught truthfully. If true history contradicts any moral we wish to teach, our moral must be wrong, and we had better abandon it. I quite admit that many people, including some of the most virtuous, find facts inconvenient, but that is due to a certain feebleness in their virtue. A truly robust morality can only be strengthened by the fullest knowledge of what really happens in the world. We must not run the risk that the young people whom we have educated in ignorance will turn to wickedness with delight as soon as they discover that there is such a thing. Unless we can give them an aversion from cruelty, they will not abstain from it; and they cannot have an aversion from it if they do not know that it exists.

Nevertheless, the right way of giving children a knowledge of evil is not easily found. Of course, those who live in the slums of big cities get to know early all about drunkenness, quarrels, wife-beating, and so on. Perhaps this does them no harm, if it is counteracted by other influences; but no careful parent would deliberately expose a very young child to such sights. I think the great objection is that they rouse fear so vividly as to colour the whole of the rest of life. A child, being defenceless, cannot help feeling terror when it first understands that cruelty to children is possible. I was about fourteen when I first read "Oliver Twist", but it filled me with emotions of horror which I could scarcely have borne at an earlier age. Dreadful things should not be known to young people until they are old enough to face them with a certain poise. This moment will come sooner with some children than with others: those who are imaginative or timid must be sheltered longer than those who are stolid or endowed with natural courage. A mental habit of fearlessness due to expectation of kindness should be firmly established before the child is made to face the existence of unkindness. To choose the moment and the manner requires tact and understanding; it is not a matter which can be decided by a rule.

There are, however, certain maxims which should be followed. To begin with, stories such as Bluebeard and Jack the Giant Killer do not involve any knowledge of cruelty whatever, and do not raise the problems we are considering. To the child, they are purely fantastic, and he never connects them with the real world in any way. No doubt the pleasure he derives from them is connected with savage instincts, but these are harmless as mere play-impulses in a powerless child, and they tend to die down as the child grows older. But when the child is first introduced to cruelty as a thing in the real world, care must be taken to choose incidents in which he will identify himself with the victim, not with the torturer. Something savage in him will exult in a story in which he identifies himself with the tyrant; a story of this kind tends to produce an imperialist. But the story of Abraham preparing to sacrifice Isaac, or of the she-bears killing the children whom Elisha cursed, naturally rouses the child's sympathy for another child. If such stories are told, they should be told as showing the depths of cruelty to which men could descend long ago. I once, as a child, heard a sermon of an hour's duration, entirely devoted to proving that Elisha was right in cursing the children. Fortunately I was old enough to think the parson a fool; otherwise I should have been driven nearly mad with terror. The story of Abraham and Isaac was even more dreadful, because it was the child's father who was cruel to him. When such stories are told with the assumption that Abraham and Elisha were virtuous, they must either be ignored or utterly debase a child's moral standards. But when told as an introduction to human wickedness, they serve a purpose, because they are vivid, remote, and untrue. The story of Hubert putting out little Arthur's eyes, in "King John", may be used in the same way.

Then history may be taught, with all its wars. But in telling about wars, sympathy at first should be with the defeated. I should begin with battles in which it is natural to feel on the side of the beaten party—for instance, the battle of Hastings in teaching an English boy. I should emphasize always the wounds and suffering produced. I should gradually lead the child to feel no partisanship in reading about wars, and to regard both sides as silly men who had lost their tempers, and ought to have had nurses to put them to bed till they were good. I should assimilate wars to quarrels among the children in the nursery. In this way, I believe children could be made to see the truth about war, and to realize that it is silly.

If any actual instance of unkindness or cruelty comes under the child's notice, it should be fully discussed, with all the moral values which the adult himself attaches to the incident, and always with the suggestion that the people who acted cruelly were foolish, and did not know any better because they had not been well brought up. But I should not call the child's attention to such things in his real world, if they were not spontaneously observed by him, until after he had grown familiar with them in history and stories. Then I should gradually introduce him to a knowledge of evil in his surroundings. But I should always give him the feeling that the evil can be combated, and results from ignorance and lack of self-control and bad education. I should not encourage him to be indignant with malefactors, but rather to regard them as bunglers, who do not know in what happiness consists.

The cultivation of wide sympathies, given the instinctive germ, is mainly an intellectual matter: it depends upon the right direction of attention, and the realization of facts which militarists and authoritarians suppress. Take, for example, Tolstoy's description of Napoleon going round the battlefield of Austerlitz after

the victory. Most histories leave the battlefield as soon as the battle is over; by the simple
expedient of lingering on it for another twelve
hours, a completely different picture of war is
produced. This is done, not by suppressing
facts, but by giving more facts. And what
applies to battles applies equally to other forms
of cruelty. In all cases, it should be quite unnecessary to point the moral; the right telling
of the story should be sufficient. Do not
moralize, but let the facts produce their own
moral in the child's mind.

It remains to say a few words about affection,
which differs from sympathy in being inevitably and essentially selective. I have spoken
already of affection between parents and children; it is affection between equals that I now
wish to consider.

Affection cannot be created; it can only be
liberated. There is a kind of affection which
is partly rooted in fear; affection for parents
has this element, since parents afford protection.
In childhood affections of this sort are natural,
but in later life they are undesirable, and even
in childhood affection for other children is not
of this sort. My little girl is intensely devoted
to her brother, although he is the only person
in her world who ever treats her unkindly.
Affection as to an equal, which is the best kind,

is much more likely to exist where there is happiness and absence of fear. Fears, conscious or unconscious, are very apt to produce hatred, because other people are regarded as capable of inflicting injuries. With most people, as things are, envy is a barrier to wide-spread affection. I do not think envy can be prevented except by happiness; moral discipline is powerless to touch its subconscious forms. Happiness, in turn, is largely prevented by fear. Young people who have a chance of happiness are deterred by parents and "friends", nominally on moral grounds, but really from envy. If the young people have enough fearlessness, they will ignore the croakers; otherwise, they will allow themselves to be made miserable, and join the company of envious moralists. The education of character that we have been considering is designed to produce happiness and courage; I think, therefore, that it does what is possible to liberate the springs of affection. More than this cannot be done. If you tell children that they ought to be affectionate, you run the risk of producing cant and humbug. But if you make them happy and free, if you surround them with kindness, you will find that they become spontaneously friendly with everybody, and that almost everybody responds by being friendly with them. A trustful affectionate disposition justifies itself, because it gives irresistible charm, and creates the response which it expects. This is one of the most important results to be expected from the right education of character.

SEX EDUCATION

THE subject of sex is so surrounded by superstitions and taboos that I approach it with trepidation. I fear lest those readers who have hitherto accepted my principles may suspect them when they are applied in this sphere; they may have admitted readily enough that fearlessness and freedom are good for a child, and yet desire, where sex is concerned, to impose slavery and terror. I cannot so limit principles which I believe to be sound, and I shall treat sex exactly as I have treated the other impulses which make up a human character.

There is one respect in which, quite independently of taboos, sex is peculiar, and that is the late ripening of the instinct. It is true, as the psycho-analysts have pointed out (though with considerable exaggeration), that the instinct is not absent in childhood. But its childish manifestations are different from those of adult life, and its strength is much less, and it is physically impossible for a boy to indulge it in the adult manner. Puberty remains an important emotional crisis, thrust into the middle of intellectual education, and causing disturbances which raise difficult problems for the educator. Many of these problems I shall not attempt to discuss; it is chiefly what should be done before puberty that I propose to consider. It is in this respect that educational reform is most needed, especially in very early childhood. Although I disagree with the Freudians in many particulars, I think they have done a very valuable service in pointing out the nervous disorders produced in later life by wrong handling of young children in matters connected with sex. Their work has already produced wide-spread beneficial results in this respect, but there is still a mass of prejudice to be overcome. The difficulty is, of course, greatly increased by the practice of leaving children, during their first years, largely in the hands of totally uneducated women, who cannot be expected to know, still less to believe, what has been said by learned men in the long words necessary to escape prosecution for obscenity.

Taking our problems in chronological order, the first that confronts mothers and nurses is that of masturbation. Competent authorities state that this practice is all but universal among boys and girls in their second and third years, but usually ceases of itself a little later on. Sometimes it is rendered more pronounced by some definite physical irritation which can be removed. (It is not my province to go into medical details.) But it usually exists even in the absence of such special reasons. It has been the custom to view it with horror, and to use dreadful threats with a view to stopping it. As a rule these threats do not succeed, although they are believed; the result is that the child lives in an agony of apprehension, which presently becomes dissociated from its original cause (now repressed into the unconscious), but remains to produce nightmares, nervousness, delusions and insane terrors. Left to itself, infantile masturbation has, apparently, no bad effect upon health[1], and no discoverable bad effect upon character; the bad effects which have been observed in both respects are, it seems, wholly attributable to attempts to stop it. Even if it were harmful, it would be unwise to issue a prohibition which is not going to be observed; and from the nature of the case, it is impossible to make sure that the child will not continue after you have forbidden him to do so. If you do nothing, the probability is that the practice will soon be discontinued. But if you do anything, you make it much less likely that it will cease, and you lay the foundation of terrible nervous disorders. Therefore, difficult as it

[1] In very rare instances, it does a little harm, but this is easily cured and is not more serious than the results of thumb-sucking.

may be, the child should be let alone in this respect. I do not mean that you should abstain from methods other than prohibition, in so far as they are available. Let him be sleepy when he goes to bed, so that he will not lie awake long. Let him have some favourite toy in bed, which may distract his attention. Such methods are quite unobjectionable. But if they fail, do not resort to prohibition, or even call his attention to the fact that he indulges in the practice. Then it will probably cease of itself.

Sexual curiosity normally begins during the third year, in the shape of an interest in the physical differences between men and women, and between adults and children. By nature, this curiosity has no special quality in early childhood, but is simply a part of general curiosity. The special quality which it is found to have in children who are being conventionally brought up is due to the grown-up practice of making mysteries. When there is no mystery, the curiosity dies down as soon as it is satisfied. A child should, from the first, be allowed to see his parents and brothers and sisters without their clothes whenever it so happens naturally. No fuss should be made either way; he should simply not know that people have feelings about nudity. (Of course, later on he will have to know.) It will be found that the child presently notices the differences between his father and mother, and connects them with the differences between brothers and sisters. But as soon as the subject has been explored to this extent, it becomes uninteresting, like a cupboard that is often open. Of course, any questions the child may ask during this period must be answered just as questions on other topics would be answered.

Answering questions is a major part of sex education. Two rules cover the ground. First, always give a truthful answer to a question; secondly, regard sex knowledge as exactly like any other knowledge. If the child asks you an intelligent question about the sun or the moon or the clouds, or about motor-cars or steam-engines, you are pleased, and you tell him as much as he can take in. This answering of questions is a very large part of early education. But if he asks you a question connected with sex, you will be tempted to say, "hush, hush". If you have learnt not to do that, you will still answer briefly and dryly, perhaps with a trifle of embarrassment in your manner. The child at once notices the *nuance*, and you have laid the foundations of prurience. You must answer with just the same fulness and naturalness as if the question had been about something else. Do not allow yourself to feel, even unconsciously, that there is something horrid and dirty about sex. If you do, your feeling will communicate itself to him. He will think, necessarily, that there is something nasty in the relations of his parents; later on, he will conclude that they think ill of the behaviour which led to his existence. Such feelings in youth make happy instinctive emotions almost impossible, not only in youth, but in adult life also.

If the child has a brother or sister born when he is old enough to ask questions about it, say after the age of three, tell him that the child grew in his mother's body, and tell him that he grew in the same way. Let him see his mother suckling the child, and be told that the same thing happened to him. All this, like everything else connected with sex, must be told without solemnity, in a purely scientific spirit. The child must not be talked to about "the mysterious and sacred functions of motherhood"; the whole thing must be utterly matter-of-fact.

If no addition to the family occurs when the child is old enough to ask questions about it, the subject is likely to arise out of being told "that happened before you were born". I find my boy still hardly able to grasp that there was a time when he did not exist; if I talk to him about the building of the Pyramids or some such topic, he always wants to know what he was doing then, and is merely puzzled when he is told that he did not exist. Sooner or later he will want to know what "being born" means, and then we shall tell him.

The share of the father in generation is less likely to come up naturally in answer to questions, unless the child lives on a farm. But it is very important that the child should know of this first from parents or teacher, not from children whom bad education has made nasty. I remember vividly being told all about it by another boy when I was twelve years old; the whole thing was treated in a ribald spirit, as a topic for obscene jokes. That was the normal experience of boys in my generation. It followed naturally that the vast majority continued through life to think sex comic and nasty, with the result that they could not respect a woman with whom they had intercourse, even though she were the mother of their children. Parents pursued a cowardly policy of trusting to luck, although fathers must have remembered how they gained their first knowledge. How it can have been supposed that such a system helped sanity or sound morals, I cannot imagine. Sex must be treated from the first as natural, delightful and decent. To do otherwise is to poison the relations of men and women, parents and children. Sex is at its best between a father and mother who love each other and their children. It is far better that children should first know of sex in the relations of their parents than that they should derive their first impressions from ribaldry. It is particularly bad that they should discover sex between their parents as a guilty secret which has been concealed from them.

If there were no likelihood of being taught badly about sex by other children, the matter could be left to the natural operation of the child's curiosity, and parents could confine themselves to answering questions—always provided that everything became known before puberty. This, of course, is absolutely essential. It is a cruel thing to let a boy or girl be overtaken by the physical and emotional changes of that time without preparation, and possibly with the feeling of being attacked by some dreadful disease. Moreover, the whole subject of sex, after puberty, is so electric that a boy or girl cannot listen in a scientific spirit, which is perfectly possible at an earlier age. Therefore, quite apart from the possibility of nasty talk, a boy or girl should know the nature of the sexual act before attaining puberty.

How long before this the information should be given depends upon circumstances. An inquisitive and intellectually active child must be told sooner than a sluggish child. There must at no time be unsatisfied curiosity. However young the child may be, he must be told if he asks. And his parents' manner must be such that he will ask if he wants to know. But if he does not ask spontaneously, he must in any case be told before the age of ten, for fear of being first told by others in a bad way. It may therefore be desirable to stimulate his curiosity by instruction about generation in plants and animals. There must not be a solemn occasion, a clearing of the throat, and an exordium: "Now, my boy, I am going to tell you something that it is time for you to know." The whole thing must be ordinary and every-day. That is why it comes best in answer to questions.

I suppose it is unnecessary at this date to argue that boys and girls must be treated alike. When I was young, it was still quite common for a "well-brought-up" girl to marry before knowing anything about the nature of marriage, and to have to learn it from her husband; but I have not often heard of such a thing in recent years. I think most people recognize nowadays that a virtue dependent upon ignorance is worthless, and that girls have the same right to knowledge as boys. If there are any who still fail to recognize this, they are not likely to read the present work, so that it is not worth while to argue with them.

I do not propose to discuss the teaching of sexual morality in the narrower sense. This is a matter as to which a variety of opinions exist.

Christians differ from Mohammedans, Catholics from Protestants who tolerate divorce, freethinkers from mediævalists. Parents will all wish their children taught the particular brand of sexual morality in which they believe themselves, and I should not wish the State to interfere with them. But without going into vexed questions, there is a good deal that might be common ground.

There is first of all hygiene. Young people must know about venereal disease before they run the risk of it. They should be taught about it truthfully, without the exaggerations which some people practise in the interests of morals. They should learn both how to avoid it, and how to cure it. It is a mistake to give only such instruction as is needed by the perfectly virtuous, and to regard the misfortunes which happen to others as a just punishment of sin. We might as well refuse to help a man who has been injured in a motoring accident, on the ground that careless driving is a sin. Moreover, in the one case as in the other, the punishment may fall upon the innocent; no one can maintain that children born with syphilis are wicked, any more than that a man is wicked if a careless motorist runs over him.

Young people should be led to realize that it is a very serious matter to have a child, and that it should not be undertaken unless the child has a reasonable prospect of health and happiness. The traditional view was that, within marriage, it is always justifiable to have children, even if they come so fast that the mother's health is ruined, even if the children are diseased or insane, even if there is no prospect of their having enough to eat. This view is now only maintained by heartless dogmatists, who think that everything disgraceful to humanity redounds to the glory of God. People who care for children, or do not enjoy inflicting misery upon the helpless, rebel against the ruthless dogmas which justify this cruelty. A care for the rights and importance of children, with all that is implied, should be an essential part of moral education.

Girls should be taught to expect that one day they are likely to be mothers, and they should acquire some rudiments of the knowledge that may be useful to them in that capacity. Of course both boys and girls ought to learn something of physiology and something of hygiene. It should be made clear that no one can be a good parent without parental affection, but that even with parental affection a great deal of knowledge is required as well. Instinct without knowledge is as inadequate in dealing with children as knowledge without instinct. The more the necessity of knowledge is understood, the more intelligent women will feel attracted to motherhood. At present, many highly educated women despise it, thinking that it does not give scope for the exercise of their intellectual faculties; this is a great misfortune, since they are capable of being the best mothers, if their thoughts were turned in that direction.

One other thing is essential in teaching about sex-love. Jealousy must not be regarded as a justifiable insistence upon rights, but as a misfortune to the one who feels it and a wrong towards its object. Where possessive elements intrude upon love, it loses its vivifying power and eats up personality; where they are absent, it fulfils personality and brings a greater intensity of life. In former days, parents ruined their relations with their children by preaching love as a duty; husbands and wives still too often ruin their relations to each other by the same mistake. Love cannot be a duty, because it is not subject to the will. It is a gift from heaven, the best that heaven has to bestow. Those who shut it up in a cage destroy the beauty and joy which it can only display while it is free and spontaneous. Here, again, fear is the enemy. He who fears to lose what makes the happiness of his life has already lost it. In this, as in other things, fearlessness is the essence of wisdom.

For this reason, in teaching my own children, I shall try to prevent them from learning a moral code which I regard as harmful. Some people who themselves hold liberal views are willing that their children shall first acquire conventional morals, and become emancipated only later, if at all. I cannot agree to this, because I hold that the traditional code not only forbids what is innocent, but also commends what is harmful. Those who have been taught conventionally will almost inevitably believe themselves justified in indulging jealousy when occasion arises; moreover they will probably be obsessed by sex either positively or negatively. I shall not teach that faithfulness to our partner through life is in any way desirable, or that a permanent marriage should be regarded as excluding temporary episodes. So long as jealousy is regarded as virtuous, such episodes cause grave friction; but they do not do so where a less restrictive morality is accepted on both sides. Relations involving children should be permanent if possible, but should not necessarily on that account be exclusive. Where there is mutual freedom and no pecuniary motive, love is good; where these conditions fail, it may often be bad. It is because they fail so frequently in the conventional marriage that a morality which is positive rather than restrictive, based upon hope rather than fear, is compelled, if it is logical, to disagree with the received code in matters of sex. And there can be no excuse for allowing our children to be taught a morality which we ourselves believe to be pernicious.

Finally, the attitude displayed by parents and teachers towards sex should be scientific, not emotional or dogmatic. For example, when it is said of a mother speaking to her daughter; "Let her tell nature's plan, *in a spirit of reverence*"; and of a father instructing his son: "The father should, in a spirit of reverence, explain nature's plan for the starting of a new life"—such sayings may be passed over by the reader as embodying nothing questionable. But to my mind there should be no more occasion for "reverence" than in explaining the construction of a steam-engine. "Reverence" means a special tone of voice from which the boy or girl infers that there is some peculiar quality about sex. From this to prurience and indecency is only a step. We shall never secure decency in matters of sex until we cease to treat the subject as different from any other. It follows that we must not advance dogmas for which there is no evidence, and which most impartial students question, such as: "After maturity is reached the ideal social relationship of the sexes is *monogamous* wedlock, to which relationship both parties should live in absolute fidelity" (ib. p. 310). This proposition may or may not be true; at present there is certainly no evidence sufficient to *prove* it true. By teaching it as something unquestionable, we abandon the scientific attitude, and do what we can to inhibit rational thought upon a most important matter. So long as this dogmatism persists in teachers, it is not to be hoped that their pupils will apply reason to any question upon which they feel strongly. And the only alternative to reason is violence.

In previous chapters, I have tried to give an outline of what can be done for the young child in the way of creating the habits which will give happiness and usefulness in later life. But I have not discussed the question whether parents are to give this training, or whether it is to be given in schools designed for the purpose. I think the arguments in favour of the nursery-school are quite overwhelming—not only for children whose parents are poor, ignorant, and overworked, but for all children, or, at the very least, for all children who live in towns. I believe that the children at Miss Margaret McMillan's nursery-school in Deptford get something better than any children of well-to-do parents can at present obtain. I should like to see the same system extended to all children, rich and poor alike. But before discussing any actual nursery-school, let us see what reasons there are for desiring such an institution.

To begin with, early childhood is of immeasurable importance both medically and psychologically. These two aspects are very closely intertwined. For example: fear will make a child breathe badly, and breathing badly will predispose it to a variety of diseases.[1] Such interrelations are so numerous that no one can hope to succeed with a child's character without some medical knowledge, or with its health without some psychology. In both directions, most of the knowledge required is very new, and much of it runs counter to time-honoured traditions. Take for example the question of discipline. The great principle in a contest with a child is: do not yield, but do not punish. The normal parent sometimes yields for the sake of a quiet life, and sometimes punishes from exasperation; the right method, to be successful, requires a difficult combination of patience and power of suggestion. This is a psychological example; fresh air is a medical example. Given care and wisdom, children profit by constant fresh air, day and night, with not too much clothing. But if care and wisdom are absent, the risk of chills from wet or sudden cold cannot be ignored.

Parents cannot be expected to possess the skill or the leisure required for the new and difficult art of dealing with young children. In the case of uneducated parents, this is obvious; they do

[1] On this subject, *cf.* "The Nursery-School", by Margaret McMillan (Dent, 1919), p. 197.

not know the right methods, and if they were taught them they would remain unconvinced. I live in an agricultural district by the sea, where fresh food is easy to obtain, and there are no extremes of heat or cold; I chose it largely because it is ideal for children's health. Yet almost all the children of the farmers, shopkeepers, and so on, are pasty-faced languid creatures, because they are indulged in food and disciplined in play. They never go to the beach, because wet feet are thought dangerous. They wear thick woollen coats out-of-doors even in the hottest summer weather. If their play is noisy, steps are taken to make their behaviour "genteel". But they are allowed to stay up late, and are given all kinds of unwholesome tit-bits of grown-up food. Their parents cannot understand why my children have not died of cold and exposure long ago; but no object lesson will convince them that their own methods are capable of improvement. They are neither poor nor lacking in parental affection, but they are obstinately ignorant owing to bad education. In the case of town parents who are poor and overworked, the evils are of course far greater.

But even in the case of parents who are highly educated, conscientious, and not too busy, the children cannot get as much of what they need as in a nursery-school. First and foremost, they do not get the companionship of other children of the same age. If the family is small, as such families usually are, the children may easily get too much attention from their elders, and may become nervous and precocious in consequence. Moreover, parents cannot have the experience of multitudes of children which gives a sure touch. And only the rich can provide the space and the environment that best suits young children. Such things, if provided privately for one family of children, produce pride of possession and a feeling of superiority, which are extraordinarily harmful morally. For all these reasons, I belive that even the best parents would do well to send their children to a suitable school from the age of two onwards, at least for part of the day—provided such a school existed in their neighbourhood.

There are, at present, two kinds of schools, according to the status of the parents. There are Froebel schools and Montessori schools for well-to-do children, and there are a small number of nursery schools for very poor children. Of the latter, the most famous is Miss McMillan's, of which the above-mentioned book gives an account which should be read by every lover of children. I am inclined to think that no existing school for well-to-do children is as good as hers, partly because she has larger numbers, partly because she is not troubled by the fussiness which middle-class snobbery obtrudes upon teachers. She aims at keeping children, if possible, from one year old till seven, though the education authorities incline to the view that the children ought to go to an ordinary elementary school at the age of five. The children come at eight in the morning, and stay till six in the evening; they have all their meals in the school. They spend as much as possible of their time out-of-doors, and indoors they have an abnormal amount of fresh air. Before a child is admitted, he or she is medically examined, and if possible cured at the clinic or in the hospital if not healthy. After admission, the children become and remain healthy with very few exceptions. There is a large, lovely garden, and a good deal of the time is spent in playing there. The teaching is broadly on Montessori lines. After dinner the children all sleep. In spite of the fact that at night, and on Sundays, they have to be in poverty-stricken homes, perhaps in cellars with drunken parents, their physique and intelligence become equal to the best that middle-class children achieve. Here is Miss McMillan's account of her seven-year-old pupils:

They are nearly all tall, straight children. All are straight, indeed, if not tall, but the average is a big, well-made child with clean skin, bright eyes, and silky hair. He or she is a little above the average of the best type of well-to-do child of the upper middle class. So much for his or her physique. Mentally he is alert, sociable, eager for life and new experience. He can read and spell perfectly, or almost perfectly. He writes well and expresses himself easily. He speaks good English and also French. He can not only help himself, but he or she has for years helped younger children: and he can count and measure and design and has had some preparation for science. His first years were spent in an atmosphere of love and calm and *fun*, and his last two years were full of interesting experiences and experiment. He knows about a garden, and has planted and watered, and taken care of plants as well as animals. The seven-year-old can dance, too, and sing and play many games. Such are the children who will soon present themselves in thousands at the Junior Schools' doors. What is to be done with them? I want to point out, first of all, that the elementary school teachers' work will be changed by this sudden uprush of clean and strong young life from below. Either the Nursery-School will be a paltry thing, that is to say a new failure, or else it will soon influence not only elementary schools but also the secondary. It will provide a new kind of children to be educated, and this must react sooner or later, not only on all the schools, but on all our social life, on the kind of government and laws framed for the people, and on the relation of our nation to other nations.

I do not think these claims exaggerated. The nursery-school, if it became universal, could, in one generation, remove the profound differences in education which at present divide the classes, could produce a population all enjoying the mental and physical development which is now confined to the most fortunate, and could remove the terrible dead-weight of disease and stupidity and malevolence which now makes progress so difficult. Under the Education Act of 1918, nursery-schools were to have been promoted by Government money; but when the Geddes Axe descended it was decided that it was more important to build cruisers and the Singapore Dock for the purpose of facilitating war with the Japanese. At the present moment, the Government is spending £650,000 a year to induce people to poison themselves with preservatives in Dominion butter and bacon rather than eat pure butter from Denmark. To secure this end, our children are condemned to disease and misery and unawakened intelligence, from which multitudes could be saved by £650,000 a year spent on nursery-schools. The mothers now have the vote; will they some day learn to use it for the good of their children? [2]

Apart from these wider considerations, what has to be realized is that the right care of young

[2] Although Miss McMillan is American, I understand that the importance of nursery-schools is even less appreciated in America than in England. As, however, there are not the financial difficulties which exist in Europe, it may be hoped that the movement will soon become widespread in the United States. There is no mention of it in O'Shea's book, though the need of it is evident from his remarks on p. 182.

children is highly skilled work, which parents cannot hope to do satisfactorily, and that it is quite different work from school-teaching in later years. To quote Miss McMillan again:

The Nursery child has a fairly good physique. Not only do his neighbours in the slums fall far short of him: his "betters" in good districts, the middle-class children, of a very good type, fall short of him. It is clear that something more than parental love and "parental responsibility" are wanted. Rules of thumb have all broken down. "Parental love" without knowledge has broken down. Child nurture has not broken down. It is very highly skilled work.

As regards the finances:

A Nursery-School of 100 children can be run to-day at an annual cost of £12 per head, and of this sum the parents in the poorest quarters can pay one-third. A Nursery-School staffed by students will cost more, but the greater part of the increased cost would be paid as fees and maintenance of future teachers. An open-air nursery and training centre, numbering in all about 100 children and thirty students, costs as nearly as makes no difference £2,200 per annum.

One more quotation:

One great result of the Nursery-School will be that the children can get faster through the curriculum of to-day. When they are half or two-thirds through the present elementary school life they will be ready to go on to more advanced work. . . . In short, the Nursery-School, if it is a *real* place of nurture, and not merely a place where babies are "minded" till they are five, will affect our whole educational system very powerfully and very rapidly. It will quickly raise the possible level of culture and attainment in all schools, beginning with the junior schools. It will prove that this welter of disease and misery in which we live, and which makes the doctor's service loom bigger than the teacher's, can be swept away. It will make the heavy walls, the terrible gates, the hard playground, the sunless and huge class-room look monstrous, as they are. It will give teachers a chance.

The nursery-school occupies an intermediate position between early training of character and subsequent giving of instruction. It carries on both at once, and each by the help of the other, with instruction gradually taking a larger share as the child grows older. It was in institutions having a similar function that Madame Montessori perfected her methods. In certain large tenement houses in Rome, a large room was set apart for the children between three and seven, and Madame Montessori was put in charge of these "Children's Houses".[3] As in Deptford, the children came from the very poorest section of the population; as in Deptford, the results showed that early

[3] See Montessori, "The Montessori Method" (Heinemann, 1912), p. 42 ff.

care can overcome the physical and mental disadvantages of a bad home.

It is remarkable that, ever since the time of Séguin, progress in educational methods with young children has come from study of idiots and the feeble-minded, who are, in certain respects, still mentally infants. I believe the reason for the necessity of this detour was that the stupidities of mental patients were not regarded as blameworthy, or as curable by chastisement; no one thought that Dr. Arnold's recipe of flogging would cure their "laziness". Consequently they were treated scientifically, not angrily; if they failed to understand, no irate pedagogue stormed at them and told them they ought to be ashamed of themselves. If people could have brought themselves to take a scientific instead of a moralizing attitude towards children, they could have discovered what is now known about the way to educate them without first having to study the mentally deficient. The conception of "moral responsibility" is "responsible" for much evil. Imagine two children, one of whom has the good fortune to be in a nursery-school, while the other is left to unalleviated slum-life. Is the second child "morally responsible" if he grows up less admirable than the first? Are his parents "morally responsible" for the ignorance and carelessness which makes them unable to educate him? Are the rich "morally responsible" for the selfishness and stupidity which have been drilled into them at expensive schools, and which make them prefer their own foolish luxuries to the creation of a happy community? All are victims of circumstances; all have had characters warped in infancy and intelligence stunted at school. No good purpose is served by choosing to regard them as "morally responsible", and holding them up to reprobation because they have been less fortunate than they might have been.

There is only one road to progress, in education as in other human affairs, and that is: Science wielded by love. Without science, love is powerless; without love, science is destructive. All that has been done to improve the education of little children has been done by those who loved them; all has been done by those who knew all that science could teach on the subject. This is one of the benefits we derive from the higher education of women: in former days, science and love of children were much less likely to coexist. The power of moulding young minds which science is placing in our possession is a very terrible power, capable of deadly misuse; if it falls into the wrong hands, it may produce a world even more ruthless and cruel than the haphazard world of nature. Children may be taught to be bigoted, bellicose, and brutal, under the pretence that they are being taught religion, patriotism, and courage, or communism, proletarianism, and revolutionary ardour. The teaching must be inspired by love, and must aim at creating love in the children. If not, it will become more efficiently harmful with every improvement in scientific technique. Love for children exists in the community as an effective force; this is shown by the lowering of the infant death-rate and the improvement of education. It is still far too weak, or our politicians would not dare to sacrifice the life and happiness of innumerable children to their nefarious schemes of bloodshed and oppression; but it exists and is increasing. Other forms of love, however, are strangely lacking. The very individuals who lavish care on children cherish passions which expose those same children, in later life, to death in wars which are mere collective insanities. Is it too much to hope that love may gradually be extended from the child to the man he will become? Will the lovers of children learn to follow their later years with something of the same parental solicitude? Having given them strong bodies and vigorous minds, shall we let them use their strength and vigour to create a better world? Or, when they turn to this work, shall we recoil in terror, and plunge them back into slavery and drill? Science is ready for either alternative; the choice is between love and hate, though hate is disguised beneath all the fine phrases to which professional moralists do homage.